# SWIPE RIGHT FOR LOVE

## Cyan LeBlanc

**Posies & Peacocks**

ISBN: 9798387651052

Cover design by: Cyan LeBlanc via Canva
Printed in the United States of America

# INTRODUCTION

This lighthearted romantic comedy was originally the brain-child of another Sapphic author, my dear friend MJ Maguire. We had planned to write the book together, but the journey fell through due to timing and other external factors. MJ passed the torch to me, and I ran with it to create a realistic look at today's dating world and how difficult it is to find your perfect soulmate while actively looking for it. Thank you, MJ, for allowing me to take us all on this journey, and I hope you and all the other readers enjoy the dangers of SWIPING RIGHT.

# SWIPE RIGHT
# FOR LOVE

# DANA

I t was what Dana referred to as a "school night," a time when she really couldn't stay out late because of the early morning wake-up call. Flowers would arrive at the butt crack of dawn, and she needed to get them processed. Nobody knew how much effort it took to keep flowers looking their best. People mistakenly believed florists simply chopped, dropped, and fluffed everything into a vase. That was not the case, especially considering that a florist had to carefully tend to the wedding flowers for an entire week in order to ensure they bloomed to their full potential. Even after she supposedly retired, her friends believed she spent every day doing nothing but playing with pretties all day.

They wanted to order another round of beers, but Dana insisted they shouldn't because she had to get up early the next day. "Seriously, guys. Tomorrow is going to come early."

"How do you expect to find someone to share your life with if you never leave your bed? You need to get out, find someone, and then get in bed with them," said Scott, Dana's flamboyant best friend who often performed in drag shows to earn a little extra spending money.

Dana's friends had encouraged her to get back out

there on the dating scene ever since she got divorced. Dana, on the other hand, thought *date* belonged in the same four-letter category as *hell*.

Dana made light of the situation by joking, "The shop is in a great location, and it is likely the ideal woman will walk right in, and voilà, instant love."

Michelle added, "Yup. That sums it up nicely. You'll once again find yourself in the role of the other woman when she's buying flowers for her girlfriend."

Michelle and Dana had been friends long before Bridgette, Dana's ex-wife, entered the picture. Although Michelle wasn't a lesbian, she knew how to appreciate a beautiful woman. She endured the most of Dana's ire and sadness after the relationship with Bridgette ended.

"Ouch! That still hurts the heart after all these years," Dana said, as her azure eyes deepened into a murky gray color while she thought about how her marriage of twenty years ended in deceit.

"You should listen to her, girlfriend. You need to be more confident in putting yourself out there." But then, as Scott continued, an idea occurred to him at that very moment. "You know, you really should get on one of those dating apps—"

Before he could complete his thought, Dana interrupted him. "No! Not going to happen."

"No. Really," Michelle agreed. "There's a new one that isn't so fishy. It's called Pryde, and it's totally gay. You know what I mean, geared toward the queer community."

At fifty-four, Dana had reached the point in her

life where the last thing she wanted was to be another notch on someone's bedpost. The stigma surrounding dating apps were that they were a cesspool for shady hookups and one-night stands. Dana wanted neither of these things in her life. "No. I'm not going to sign up for a dating site so that people can glance at my picture and decide whether I'm worthy of a quick roll in the hay. I'll find love the old-fashioned way: by chance meeting, having lunch, and falling in love. Fifty-four is too old for that dating nonsense."

After a few more drinks and the persistent prodding of her friends, Dana finally gave in and downloaded the Pryde app. If nothing else, she wanted to see what all the fuss was about. Scott and Michelle huddled up next to her as she filled out the registration form and checked the box indicating that she accepted the terms of service. They browsed through a few public and sponsored profiles before creating Dana's profile page. Dana couldn't fathom why anyone would want to sponsor a profile so prominent, unless they were extremely desperate or took having one-night stands to a competition level.

They chortled and laughed at a few of the accounts, making snide comments about some obscene profile photos and kinky descriptions of their activities. After reading a woman preferred blondes with double D breasts, Dana flung down her phone in disgust. "No. I can't do this."

"These are the extremes. There will always be these types of people. We need to create a profile for you, then let the algorithms do their thing. It's a science." Michelle reached over the table and retrieved her friend's phone, which she returned to her.

"Fine." Dana accepted it and followed the instructions by clicking the link to begin her questionnaire. "What are my kinks?"

As Scott continued down the list, he voiced his opinion by saying, "Oo. Latex."

Dana cringed. "I don't even know what it means, but yeah, no. Kissing, I guess. Looking–,"

Michelle intervened and prevented Dana from clicking that button. "Wait! Don't click that, it might mean you want to watch other people."

"I don't even know what half this stuff means. They built this for a millennial with all their made-up terms. I'm not into feet or furries. What the hell does NSA mean? The only things that sound remotely like me are monogamy and vanilla."

"What? You're not into tentacles?" Scott laughed.

"I don't even want to know." Dana selected the three options that presented the least risk on the screen. When Dana was on the verge of clicking the next button, Michelle tapped the button that said *oral*. Dana glared at her friend.

"What? It's what you do."

Dana left the box checked and clicked next. "Hobbies? Perfect. Those are easy." With a few taps, Dana chose art, cooking, hiking, music, and theater.

Scott had an opinion based on the options given. "Do not choose naps, please."

"But I enjoy sleeping." Dana smiled but refrained from clicking the button. She didn't particularly enjoy doing it; it was more of a chore than a pastime for her. Next. "Personality?"

Michelle chose for her. "Chill, confident, fun, mature, and dependable."

Dana gave Michelle the side eye as she asked, "So, you don't think I'm loyal? Because I was more than loyal to Bridgette. I stayed with her for far too long. And what about romantic?"

"You aren't a dog. Loyalty is overrated, especially when she's sleeping with everyone in a skirt. This time, you should be less loyal." Michelle told it like it was and never sugarcoated over negative issues. She'd pushed for Dana's divorce when she recognized the telltale signs of Bridgette's infidelity a long time before Dana accepted the truth about her former wife.

"Fine. What's next?" The next question was a list of other options and tags to include. "College, cuddling, drug-free, friends, lesbian, and no smoking." She checked with her friends, still huddled together next to her, before pressing the next button. With affirmative nods from each of them, she moved on to the following step.

The following screen contained the description of her profile. Before beginning the three hundred character summary of her life and identity, she took a deep breath. How was it possible for her to summarize who she was in just a few sentences?

She began speaking it out loud while simultaneously typing it. "I'm Dana, fifty-four years old, and a lesbian–"

"Are you in a lesbian support group?" Scott

grabbed her phone and started typing his thoughts. "Middle-aged hottie seeking stimulating conversation, friendship, and love—"

Michelle pulled the phone away from Scott. "I swear, it sounds like a want ad in the newspaper. Let me do this."

She dashed her fingers across the screen, making it impossible for Dana to look over her shoulder. Michelle hid the screen from them. When she finished, she placed the phone upside down on the table. Michelle gave Dana a smack on the hand as she reached for it. "Stop. Trust me. Leave the matchmaking to the machines, and if you don't have a couple of connections in a few days, you can return to your lesbian's anonymous profile."

Dana accepted the profile should remain unchanged, but she continued to reach for her phone. When Michelle gave her a dirty look, Dana defended herself by giving her another. "I said, fine. I've stayed here longer than I intended, and I really must get up early tomorrow. Let me know how much I owe you for the drinks, and I'll send you cash in the morning."

She nudged Scott from the booth so that she could leave. She blew kisses to both of them as she strolled away. Dana opened the bar's front door, slamming right into a female police officer on her way in.

While still wearing her uniform, the law enforcement officer of Latin descent apologized, "I'm sorry. Excuse me."

On her way out, Dana glanced over her shoulder, giving the officer another look. Even though she had no desire to find a romantic partner, she wasn't dead. Dana appreciated a stunning and self-assured woman. The officer appeared to fulfill both requirements. Dana sighed and smiled slyly as she made her way to her car, all the while entertaining the idea of using the handcuffs on that police officer.

The course of her life had been one unexpected event after another. She started working at the investment banking firm right after she graduated from college. She became one of the youngest vice presidents at the company. Meeting Bridgette was also entirely coincidental. Dana volunteered to take over for one of her coworkers, who had to step down after making a huge mistake that almost lost a client. She put in a ton of late nights, combing through the financial records with Bridgette. From their first kiss, they continued a passionate romance that lasted twenty years. Despite Bridgette's well-earned reputation for being a heartbreaker, Dana felt optimistic about them living happily ever after. That was, until Dana caught Bridgette kissing one of her female coworkers during a late night conference, proving Bridgette lived up to the reputation she had earned.

After the divorce, Dana discovered another unexpected interest in life: she loved being a florist. What she considered being a hobby of going to the grocery store or a local flower shop, picking out some lovely blooms, and designing them in her own vases turned into friends and family asking her to provide flowers for parties and weddings. She recognized her talent for it and made the decision that, rather than working in an office, she would indulge her creative side. Opening a flower shop had been the best decision she ever made. It brought her much joy. What she lacked in her life was someone to come home to at night, someone to cook a delicious meal for, someone to cuddle up with on the couch, and, of course, someone to sleep next to in bed.

Perhaps the next unexpected life event would be the discovery of another great love, matched by an algorithm designed by a pimple-nosed geek in Silicon Valley. What better way to express your feelings for someone than to swipe left or right on their profile picture? The idea of using a dating app sounded even less appealing than the archaic practice of going on blind dates, even though friends usually vetted those dates. It was not safe nor sane to agree to meet someone based solely on a few photos and a three-hundred-word character profile.

Her phone rang with the alert as she drove home. She opened it expecting a text message, but to her surprise, it was the app. It had found another user with similar interests. While laughing, Dana tossed the phone on the passenger seat of the car. By the time she arrived at her house, quite a few people had viewed her profile, and it had received three likes.

She sat down on the couch, pulled up the app on her phone, and began perusing the profiles of the people who had liked hers. Helen, a stout woman of sixty-five years with an enormous gap between her teeth, appeared on her screen. She recoiled in horror.

She hated the idea of appearing shallow, but she couldn't see herself with that woman. The photos failed to pique her interest, so she slid to the left and declined to accept the match. If dating apps were a game of falling in love with a photo, she would play it intelligently.

Kimberly, a young woman of twenty-six years, was the second person who expressed an interest. She was adorable, but Dana chose not to consider her based on her age. According to the profile, Kimberly wanted a grandmother figure. Dana swept her hand subconsciously across her graying temples. Another swipe to the left because Dana couldn't picture herself with someone whose profile said she got off to grannies. Finally, a woman who reminded Dana of Bridgette gave the final like of the evening. The photograph depicted Jana in a business suit with a low-cut neckline for her profile. Jana exuded sophistication and class, which arched Dana's brow with interest.

According to her online dating profile, Jana was 49 years old, had a soft spot for pooches, and hunted for a second chance at love. There was no evidence that pointed to a serial killer in her photos. One of which showed Jana cuddling with a dog, and another of her wearing a baseball cap. *What could it hurt?*

Dana swiped right on her potential interest in meeting Janna. Tossing the phone to the side, she sighed and leaned back on the couch. Mr. Jinx jumped onto her lap and curled himself into a ball just as she unwound. "Yup, I know Jinx. I want someone to curl up with too. But until then, let's go to bed. Tomorrow will come incredibly early."

Dana picked up her furry child and carried him to their bedroom, where they spent the night huddled under the covers.

The morning arrived much too quickly. The sound of Dana's alarm caused her to groan, and she silently berated her friends for keeping her out much later than she should have. She dragged herself out of the house without even taking a shower and made it to the flower shop in time to meet her floral wholesaler before the sun rose above the horizon. She tore into the boxes, removing the bunches of garden roses, standard roses, butterfly ranunculus, anemones, and hydrangea. Dana took a long whiff of one of the heritage garden rose blooms because she adored the fragrance. It reminded her of a beautiful peony, but they were out of season. Peonies were something the customer fervently desired to include in her bouquet. Instead, they settled for the stunning pink English garden rose as a compromise.

As she placed the roses in the chemical ladened water, her phone rang. She wrinkled her brow at the sound and wondered who needed her at that hour. At such an early hour, no one should need her unless it was an employee calling in sick. She pulled out her phone to find the annoying dating app sent the notification. She scowled, then slammed it down on the table again. Dana paused. Did she see that right?

When she picked up her phone again, there

were eleven different notifications from the app. She immediately wondered what in the hell Michelle wrote on her profile that would compel eleven different people to like it. She did not bother to look at the candidates; rather, she tapped the screen until she found her profile and read it.

*Ladies, I'm single and ready to mingle. Let's get out of the house and have some fun. Swipe and let's chat.*

Dana sputtered, grabbed her chest, and came dangerously close to choking. Michelle made it sound as though Dana wanted nothing more than a one-night stand. That was precisely the opposite of what she wanted.

A connection; the experience of falling in love. That had a lovely ring to it. The epitome of lesbian culture was being single and ready to mingle. Every single television show portrayed lesbian women as easy and engaging in sexual activities with whoever they pleased. Dana tapped the "edit" button on her phone just as another tone rang out from the app. Dana reconsidered and switched over to the newly alerted profile, where she saw a woman with gorgeous eyes and shoulder-length, light brown hair. She stared at the picture for a while, intent on discovering a flaw in the woman's appearance.

What did she imagine she would find when she signed up for a dating service? People addicted to meth with missing teeth. Dana swiped right without reading the profile to save her for later consideration. Work needed to come first. Dana hung up her phone and cranked up the tunes on the store's stereo while she danced around the store and played with the pretties.

Dana eventually stopped long enough to grab a bite to eat around lunchtime. She went to her office, which was a tiny nook with just enough space for a chair and a desk. Her laptop sat on the desk, which she pushed to the side for her brown-bag lunch. She pulled her phone from the pocket of her pants while she ate her sandwich and potato chips. Once more, she noticed several notifications from the app saying she had a lot of interested followers.

She did not check them, instead she dialed Michelle's number. As soon as Michelle answered, Dana declared, "I am not ready to mingle!"

On the other end of the phone, Michelle laughed. "Did it work? Any biters?"

Dana buried her head in her hand. "I am fairly certain that many of the hundred alerts want to bite me. I need to update my profile. You made me sound like I just wanted to get laid."

"But don't you want to get laid?"

The color drained from her face, and she turned away from the door to hide it. Dana lowered her voice intentionally so that her employee wouldn't hear. "Yes, but not at the expense of my dignity. That's why I have Big Bertha."

"Believe me, a human is far superior to a battery-boyfriend. In your case, girlfriend. Go on a few dates, and if you discover that it's more about quantity than quality, you can change your profile. Give it a shot, girl. So, how many likes did you receive?"

Dana's voice dropped even lower as she grumbled out the number, "Thirty-two."

"Oh, shit! Maybe you should change your profile."

Dana took a bite out of her sandwich, then continued speaking with food in her mouth. "I warned you. A few looked promising, but I haven't had time to go through them all."

"Choose one or two that seem interesting and contact them. Let me know how it turns out. I want all the juicy details."

"There will be no juicy details. I seriously doubt quality people will use a dating app."

"You're using a dating app. Are you quality? Perhaps they are women like you who have friends pressuring them to date again."

"Fine. Whatever. I'll message someone."

Even after Dana agreed to use the app, hoping to meet someone, she still carried a healthy amount of skepticism with her throughout the day at work. Just a few minutes before the end of day, she questioned Miguel, the designer working for her, if he had ever used a dating app.

"Of course, Mami." He spoke with a Latin accent and made flamboyant hand gestures as he announced, "I got a date tonight with a Mister who is quite tasty."

Dana asked, "Which app do you use?"

"Oh, I's got them all. You thinking 'bout finding a hot misses?"

She bit her lips together to suppress her laughter.

"I don't know about hot. Have you heard of an app called Pryde?"

"Yes. Yes. It's a good one. Lots of hotties."

She couldn't help but laugh at Miguel's assumption that anyone who walked past him was already hot or someone he could make hot by dressing them up. "Don't laugh, but I joined Pryde and already have a few hits. Are they referred to as hits? Likes? Or whatever, but some people liked my profile, but I wouldn't classify them as hotties."

"Lemme see."

Miguel walked alongside her as Dana opened her phone so that they could make snap judgments about the content of a book based solely on its cover. Dana's perspective on the dating scene in today's technologically advanced world reminded her of online shopping for books. One or two photographs were the cover art, and they used three hundred words as the blurb. A summary of bullet points offered the greatest possibility of persuading someone to read the entire story.

As they pulled up Jana's profile, he leaned into her personal space. Miguel looked at the photograph with his nose scrunched up, he stated, "No. I say no to this one."

"Why? She's a little strong, but she's wearing a business suit and has puppies. What's the matter with her?"

"The clothes are fake. Lookie." He pointed to a dot on the screen. "Store tags. She's in a dressing room. The undershirt doesn't even match. You miss all details."

"What about the cute dog?" Dana asked, not wanting to give up hope.

"No. No. She's at an adoption. Look at backgrounds. It's all staged. She wants your body, not your romance. Skip her." Miguel, unwavering in his evaluation, tapped the screen to disagree with the heart that Dana had given to Jana.

The decision-making process for selecting a date left her feeling overwhelmed. The knot forming in her stomach gave rise to uncertainty in her mind. She did not notice the subtle clues that pointed to a fake person. She quickly took her phone away from him. "I'm just going to remove this. It's a total waste of time."

"Ay, no, Mami. It's not. We find you some spicy ones that will rock your socks. I promise."

While Miguel appeared optimistic that he would find someone who was ideal for her, Dana felt the complete opposite. It was possible the pessimistic outlook she had toward the entire process prevented her from being open to the possibility of a new romantic partnership. Miguel guided her through selecting some promising candidates while simultaneously assisting her in evading the trolls. By the time they finished scrolling through her likes, she discovered some her own based on her own preferences.

Miguel walked out of the store as Dana waved goodbye and closed it up. When she finished locking up, she turned her attention to the edge of the strip center. Two police cars sat with their lights flashing. The sudden appearance of a female officer startled her, especially with her heightened apprehension of the presence of law enforcement.

When Dana jumped, the police officer greeted her with a friendly smile and reassured her there was nothing frightening going on down there. "Just a speeder that we pulled over."

"That's helpful to know." Dana pulled her hand away from her chest after she had drawn it toward her while she gasped for air.

"A flower shop, huh? I'll have to pay you a visit. My mother's birthday is coming up in a few months."

After gazing at the officer's friendly face for a moment, Dana's eyes shifted downward. Instead of focusing on her breasts, which were hidden by her bulletproof vest, she noticed the name tag. Morales. Just then, she made the connection. Morales was the same officer who entered the bar as she exited the night before. "Well, Officer Morales. We offer a police discount, so stop by whenever you want. I'll make something lovely for your mother."

"Thanks. Sure will." Officer Morales kept walking in the direction of the police vehicles parked at the far end of the strip.

Dana found Morales appealing, but she couldn't bring herself to ask a uniformed woman out on a date. She shrugged it off as unimportant and finished locking up. In the split second it took for her to duck her head inside the vehicle and slam the door shut, a notification appeared on her phone. She received a message through the Pryde app from a user. Dana opened it with a grin and a light chuckle. To her surprise, it was a message from the woman Miguel chose for her.

# ABIGAIL

*Abs here. New to Orlando. Butch. Gym Rat.
Harley Rider. Tattoo Lover. Looking for a femme
with no kids. Pets OK. Someone who likes the
outdoors, healthy, and absolutely... no smoking.*

**D**ana made her way through the photos
of Abigail. Abigail's appearance was more
masculine androgynous than Dana was
comfortable with; she had dark, curly hair on top with
the sides of her head shaved down to the scalp. Her
clear blue eyes were the same color as the summer sky
in Orlando. They captured Dana's attention at once.
The following picture showed the same woman on
the beach. She had a six-pack of chiseled abdominal
muscles. Perhaps that was why she referred to her as
*Abs*. It was impossible for Dana to deny that Abs had
a stunningly beautiful and fit body. The tattoos on her
arms accentuated her shape; not detract from it.

She read the profile, evaluating herself along
the way. Even though Dana was not traditionally
feminine, she could be girly when the occasion

demanded it. Other than Mr. Jinx, she did not have any children. Dana considered herself to be healthy, although she did not have a six-pack and had a little meat on her bones. Most of which came from drowning her sorrows in chocolate ice cream. She enjoyed a day out in the fresh air. Besides that, she was not a smoker, either. In getting back into the dating game, Abigail wasn't a terrible first choice.

When Dana finally got home, she made some dinner for herself and a bowl of tuna for Mr. Jinx before settling in for the night. She responded to Abigail's generic greeting with a message of her own. Abigail's response came within a few moments, and the two of them communicated throughout the night via text messages.

Abs, as she preferred to be called, didn't give off the impression of being superficial. Dana gave Abigail her phone number. She'd rather continue the conversation on a more personal level. However, the messages continued. The only difference was they didn't use the app but sent messages directly to each other.

They settled on a get together the following night at a bar, rather close to the city's nightlife. Abigail selected the location. Even though Dana didn't mind the drive, she would have preferred to meet at her neighborhood pub.

Before calling it a night, Dana called Michelle and provided a comprehensive account of her interaction with Abigail and the topics they discussed. Dana's best friend gave her the green light to go out on this first date, which boosted her confidence.

As she locked the door to her flower shop the following day, a text message from Abigail rang her phone. The note explained Abigail needed to cancel that night's planned dinner date. After a trying day, during which a bridezilla kept complaining the Quicksand roses were too pink for her taste, Dana exhaled a sigh of relief and thanked her lucky stars. Flowers didn't always play nice with mother nature, a concept that brides didn't quite understand.

As soon as Dana got inside her house, she fled straight for the couch and collapsed. Mr. Jinx leaped onto her lap and nuzzled her. "I know you missed me. At the very least, I'll be spending the night with you. You can hate me tomorrow when I go out."

With soft music in the background, she changed into her comfiest pajamas and poured herself a glass of Pinot Noir. Dana threw onions and peppers into a hot pan as she swayed to the music of blues royalty, Bessie Smith. Her stomach growled, thinking about the chicken that spent an entire day soaking up the flavorful red wine sauce. As she dropped the chicken into the pan with the veggies, her phone rang again.

After quickly cleaning her hands, she grabbed her phone and read the message.

*Hi. I'm sorry again. My appointment got canceled, so I have problems with tomorrow now. Could we please keep our evening date? I've been looking forward to meeting you all day, and I'd hate to wait another week.*

Dana gave a shrug, knowing things happened. She

turned the chicken over carefully so as not to ruin what she had been craving for the past few days. She set the date with Abigail much more quickly than expected, but seeing as how Michelle and Miguel were on board with it, she put her faith in them. Dana longed for the days when people courted each other and took the time to get to know one another through their actions and mannerisms. Her previous relationship happened by a chance encounter at work, which led to a spark between them. She still found verbal conversation more meaningful than reading tiny text on a screen.

She responded to the message after removing the pan from the stove and setting it aside.

*Sure. Let's make it a little later though. I'll have to get ready. Let's say 8 p.m.?*

On the screen appeared an emoji of a thumbs up. She winced at Abigail's inability to answer innocuously with "yes" or "I'll see you there."

Setting the time for eight o'clock allowed her to enjoy the delectable chicken dish she prepared. At the table, she took the first bite with a sigh of contentment. "I'll have to try more dishes from this website."

When Dana arrived at the pub, she cast a cursory glance in every direction to find Abigail. Dana assumed she was still waiting for her date because she was early rather than prompt or late. She quickly communicated to Abigail her intention to find a table by sending a text message. She received a response.

*Great. I'm in the bathroom. Order me a Goose Island IPA. Be out in a sec.*

She located a booth relatively close to the entrance and placed the drink order there while she waited. And continued to wait. And wait. The hostess brought out the chilled glasses.

When Abigail sat down on the bench opposite her with a sheepish grin on her face, Dana was already halfway through her beer. "Geez. I am truly sorry about that. Dude, I must have eaten something that didn't agree with me at lunch," Abigail said, then downed half of her beer in one gulp. "I had to sit back down every time I got out off the pot and flushed."

Dana's eyes narrowed as she hid her gasp. "Perhaps we should reschedule?"

"Nonsense. I think I'm all set now. Unless I get up and start running." Abigail laughed and continued. "Sorry about earlier. My brother broke up with his girlfriend today, and it devastated him. I canceled because he wanted me to spend the evening with him. Then he decided to go barhopping with his mates to cheer himself up, reopening my evening. The next few days would have been even more disastrous. I'm going on a ride with a couple of friends tomorrow. You know, those dykes on bikes. We would have had to reschedule for next week, but I really wanted to meet you. You look a little different in your online photos. Obviously not completely different, because I recognized you. In the photos, your hair was a little longer."

Because of how much Abigail rambled, Dana

waited before saying anything. Her date didn't even greet her or thank her for ordering her beer, which bothered her. When there was finally an opening, Dana said, "That was from last year. I don't believe I've changed all that much."

"You look better with longer hair. So, my brother's girlfriend had the audacity to cheat on him with a coworker. He works at a restaurant near Universal Studios. We should go there because it is both delicious and healthy. There isn't a lot of processed food. Most of the food is farm to table."

Dana sat with her palm under her chin and her elbow on the table, listening to Abigail tell another story. Abigail made a show of waving her hand around in exaggerated gestures as she continued on. "Now, about the girl. She told him this morning that she had to sleep with this guy because she lost a bet. But after sleeping with him, she realized it was a stupid bet, especially since my brother was much better in bed. I mean, really? Why would you say something like that in the first place?"

Dana pushed her lips together and shook her head, unable to decide whether she should respond or not. Abigail didn't even wait for Dana to answer before going on with what she was saying. "I think my brother might come by. They were going from bar to bar, and I told them where we would be. I hope that's okay. Unless they're already drunk, they're pretty chill."

"No. The more the merrier." That was a lie. Dana didn't want anyone else to join them on their date, which wasn't going well to begin with. Could she really tell this woman she hardly knew that she didn't want her newly single brother to join them?

At that very moment, three rowdy guys burst into the pub, laughing and falling all over each other. Abigail said, "Glad you're cool with it. Here they are."

Dana glanced over her shoulder again, watching them stumbling toward the booth. Abigail stood up and waved them over. The guys sat on the other side of the booth, and Abigail switched sides to sit next to Dana, who moved to make room. More like Abigail pushed Dana with her hips to shove her aside.

When Dana felt a hand on her thigh, she immediately looked down at her leg. Her expression changed at Abigail's audacity to be that forward. Sweat beaded on the small of her back as she tried to ignore the obnoxious guys across from her and the woman touching her inappropriately next to her. She no longer could get away from this spiraling date.

Dana scooted over and gently removed Abigail's hand from her leg. When Abigail's hand slipped off Dana's leg, Abs lifted her arm, wrapped it around Dana's shoulder, and pulled her close. "This is Dana, guys."

The rowdy, already drunk men waved and hollered, laughing about something Dana didn't seem to understand. Abigail introduced them to her. "This is my brother, Charlie."

Dana smiled half-heartedly, gave him a polite nod, and mouthed the words "hello" to him.

"And these are his mates, Kennedy and Ernie."

Ernie, friendlier than the others, put out his hand for Dana to shake. Dana wasn't rude, so she shook it while Charlie spoke. "No offense, Dana, but Abs, after what Emma did to me, are you sure you want to start dating? Seriously, women are bitches."

Abigail laughed with her arm draped around Dana's neck as she held on tightly. Not only did Charlie's offensive comments contribute to a stereotypically derogatory view of women, but Abigail laughed with them instead of stepping up to defend women in general.

Dana twisted her head in anticipation of seeing Abigail knock her brother down two levels. Instead, Abigail grinned. "I like bitches, especially ones in heat."

As she finished that sentence, she leaned into Dana as if Dana were the one yearning for some sexual favor. That wasn't the case at all. Dana, who had finally had enough, pushed Abigail out of the booth and whispered she needed to use the restroom.

Abigail called out to Dana as she left, "Don't take too long, babe!"

Dana let out an audible gasp. She laughed to herself and rolled her eyes at the whole situation she found herself in. She forced her way into the filthy restroom, which needed a significant amount of deep cleaning from the staff of the bar. At the last stall, she cringed. A smeared line of white powder sat atop the toilet tank. Backed up with feces, the bowl sat full and smelled.

She moved to the next available stall. Much the

same. At that point, she decided she wouldn't even attempt to find a clean one. Instead, she washed her hands and pondered her options while at the sink. Dana peered upward at the mirror in front of her. She was better than this and needed a way out of the situation. No matter which way she fled, she would have to pass the table on her way out. They'd notice her leaving.

When the door opened with some significant force, Dana immediately directed her attention to it. Abigail plowed right on through it. "Hey, babe. You okay in here?"

Suppressing a laugh, Dana said, "Yep, just washing up."

Abigail pulled a small bag out of her pocket and held it up with a little jiggle. She showed it to Dana. A white powdery substance waved in the air. "Wanna hit?"

Dana's jaw dropped as she couldn't believe it. The entire date was going to shit. She declined with a shake of her head. Finally, when Dana formed a few choice words for her date, the three guys busted through the door looking for Abigail.

"Thanks for inviting us to the party." Charlie grabbed the bag from Abigail and pushed through the last stall with his friends.

"You coming?" Abigail held out her hand toward Dana.

Dana replied as nicely as she could, "You know, this isn't really my scene. I think I'll leave."

"Come on, don't go. Let them play. We'll go back

outside and chat. I really like you."

Dana waved her hand in the air to say that she wasn't interested. "Look, this really isn't going well. Charlie's break up. The guys. I'm just going to call it a night."

Abigail moved forward. Her bold moves intruded on Dana's space. She grabbed Dana's arms and pulled her forward, but Dana resisted. That move seemed to offend Abigail. "What? I don't get a kiss goodnight?"

Dana took a step back. "I'm sorry. Call me old-fashioned, but I don't do that on the first date."

The comment surprised Abigail. She threw up her hands, obviously fed up with her. "You don't need to be a bitch about it."

Dana took another step back and widened her eyes in confusion. "Excuse me? I'm not the one being a bitch about anything. I came to this place to meet someone nice. Most of my dates don't involve rude men and drugs, thank you very much."

She swung on her heel, strode out of the restroom, and prepared to leave. Dana made a quick pit stop at the bar, where she spoke to the bartender while leaning over the counter. Dana threw her a ten-dollar bill and said, "Abigail will pay the bill, but I don't think they're the kind of people who leave tips, so take this just in case."

Dana placed her cell phone to her ear when she walked out the front door of the bar. When Michelle answered, Dana said, "That's it. I'm done with this dating app and everything about it."

It took a lot of convincing from Michelle, but by the end of the night, Dana gave in to Michelle's request. She agreed to play the dating game, writing off her awful date with Abigail as a fluke. Dana made a mental note to conduct more thorough research before going out on the next one, including inquiring if the other person used illegal substances. She never in her right mind thought she'd have to ask that question right off the bat. Times had certainly changed since the last time she dated.

# BRITT

*Originally from Austin, TX. Moved to Orlando recently. Looking for someone to enjoy a good movie, fine foods, and intelligent conversation. Gemini. 42. Blogger.*

Dana didn't pay attention to the app or any of the messages she received until the wedding was over for the week. She had to concentrate on the source of her income, which was bridezillas with Karens for mothers.

As she completed the flower arch from a ladder, she murmured to Miguel, "Remind me never to mention these darn floral arches again."

In his thick accent, Miguel replied, "You say that every single time you make one, and every single time, I remind you."

"Yeah, I know. Don't remind me you remind me every time." They both giggled as Dana climbed down from the ladder.

The mother of the bride walked through the arch with another woman, muttering, "I still think these roses are excessively pink, but whatever. It will suffice. I'll have the photographer adjust the color in Photoshop."

As soon as the women disappeared behind the wall, Dana clenched her fists into tight balls and shook them in the air. "It's f-ing mother nature, woman. I've said this a million and eighty-seven times."

"Bruja!" Miguel cursed, causing Dana to chuckle at his name calling in Spanish. He swiftly shifted the subject, but it was not the one Dana desired. "So any new chihuahuas this weekend for you?"

"God, no! After that one, I need a break, though I made a commitment to Michelle that I wouldn't give up on this too soon."

"No, you don't quit on love. Gimme your phone. I look for a good one." Miguel put his hand out. Dana gave Miguel her phone with a laugh, and Miguel swiped left a few times until he held it up to her. A picture of a beautiful woman. Britt was her name. Cute. Liked movies a lot. Miguel said, "I swiped her for you. You send love note and bam! You go on date."

Dana laughed as she took back her phone and typed: *Hi. I'm Dana. Saw you liked movies. We have something in common. So do I. If you'd like to chat, send me a message.*

It was a straightforward message. Generic enough so it didn't send a hook up vibe. Ideally, just enough interest to capture the reader's curiosity. Dana was not the type of person to go overboard in her admiration for a cute person. When Dana finally arrived at her house, she found Britt had already sent her a message.

*White Chicks* was Dana's go-to choice for a good

laugh, so she settled in for a movie with Mr. Jinx. She would have played *Fried Green Tomatoes* if she wanted an emotional cry. A comedy provided the ideal accompaniment to a night spent texting Britt. They enjoyed themselves during the chat, and by the time it was through, they confirmed a get together the following day for lunch.

She entered the café under the impression she would have time to spare before her date. Despite being ten minutes early, Dana was not the first to arrive. Britt greeted Dana with a wave. By Britt arriving early, it set a positive tone for the date. Dana shuffled her way to the table, where Britt stood and gave a proper handshake.

"Please sit. I hope the table is okay. We could move if you don't enjoy sitting by the door," Britt offered with a point toward the back of the café.

Dana said, "This is perfect. I actually like sitting by the door."

They both said simultaneously, "Escape route!"

Dana laughed, her lips pursed. "Not that I need one, but it's useful to have, especially on a first date."

"I wholeheartedly concur. I've gone on a few awful dates that have made me doubt dating all together."

Hearing Britt's statements helped lessen the tension because Dana experienced many of the same emotions, although she had only gone on one date since her divorce from Bridgette. After the first awkwardness passed, the two women asked each other the fundamental questions about dating, such as who they were, where they were from, and a little about their past relationships. Dana's stomach had been full of butterflies since she woke up, but the ebb and flow of their conversation helped settle them down, even if she continued to have a pessimistic outlook. The shit could hit the fan at any time.

Britt discussed her childhood years and her family life in Austin, Texas. Dana leaned in to the talk, actively participating but maintaining a comfortable demeanor. She intently scrutinized the woman sitting opposite of her. Her hair was dark and shoulder-length, and styled in a feathery backwards bob. Her brown eyes really stood out because of the eyeliner. She only used a little shadow on the outer corners. In contrast to Dana's classic lesbian appearance, Britt radiated with alluring femininity. The longer Dana stared, the more uncomfortable she became with how she appeared to others. Although Dana was content with her appearance as it was, she couldn't shake the nagging feeling that she ought to have made more of an effort to appear more attractive.

Britt was mid-sentence when the waitress arrived with their order. When they were finally by themselves, Britt stated, "I feel as though I have dominated the entire conversation. What prompted your divorce? I mean, twenty years is a long time to just throw it away."

Dana avoided discussing Bridgette as much as possible. The breakup of her marriage hurt her deeply, no matter how much time had passed. When Dana married Bridgette, she did it with the utmost faith in the vows. Forever meant until death. She intended to retire and spend her golden years alongside her wife. Dana exhaled deeply and stated, "I wasn't the one who threw it away. My ex didn't seem to have a single faithful bone in her body. Because my friends witnessed it, perhaps I am not a good judge of character. I closed my eyes to avoid seeing the inevitable."

"Well, I think you are because you chose me." Britt smiled as she touched Dana's hand from across the table.

Dana experienced a sense of serenity throughout her body because of the warmth of her touch. They clasped hands with one another. Both of their eyes and smiles met, and they stayed like that until the quiet loomed over the table. When the need to kiss Britt came over Dana, she formed a thin line with her lips and waited for it to pass. Instead of allowing the natural connection to occur, she abruptly withdrew her hand.

Dana changed the subject. "Your profile said you're a movie lover. What's your favorite movie?"

Britt laughed whole-heartedly. "That is a loaded question, especially considering I'm a professional film critic. Comparable to asking Ebert what his favorite film is. When you've watched more than the typical person, it's difficult to choose just one."

Dana, the average person, found the question to be simple, although she did not understand what Ebert meant. "I love *Fried Green Tomatoes*. Oh, and *The Piano*."

Britt leaned on the table and folded her hands in front of her. "The thought of having a favorite film strikes me as pretentious. There are two types of film enthusiasts: fan boys and appreciators. Fan boys will argue endlessly about their preferred films and directors. Particularly, directors. As if they believe Tarantino is the ultimate filmmaker and none of his films are bad."

Dana could only nod as she listened closely while Britt's eyes expanded and sparkled as she spoke about movies.

"Film aficionados will watch everything, take in all the cinematic elements, and evaluate the film as a whole. Here is where I fall with films. There are films I feel everyone, including the ordinary moviegoer, has seen. They are classics. We will remember them as some of the best films of all time, and those who haven't seen them are idiots. *Vertigo. Citizen Kane. Jaws. Casablanca.*"

Dana interjected, "I guess I am an idiot because I've never seen *Jaws.*"

The table grew silent as Britt's gaze sharpened. As the attitude shifted, heat emanated from across the table. "You've never seen *Jaws*?"

Dana responded with a shake of her head, "I'm not a huge fan of horror films."

Britt sat up tall with her chest puffed out, her backbone erect. "*Jaws* is not horror. Literally, it is the tale of a misunderstood and misaligned fish who faces off against a drunken fisherman. Jaws is an excellent film, and not just because Spielberg directed it. It is an allegory for *Moby-Dick*. How have you never seen *Jaws*? I am not being pretentious in the least."

Dana dismissed the matter. "I've never been interested in watching it."

Britt became so perplexed by Dana's lack of interest in a movie that she stopped speaking and merely shook her head in disgust. She shifted her head and stared away from the table, as if she could no longer look Dana in the eyes. Dana remarked once again, "You know, I'll check to see if it's available on streaming when I get home and give it a go. I mean, I would hate to miss such a terrific film."

As she spoke, Britt withdrew her phone from her purse and touched the screen. "There is an app for that. Let me see." She returned her phone to her purse. "There is no streaming available. You will just have to come over to watch it."

Dana giggled to herself quietly as she realized what that meant: Britt wanted a second date. Although they did not share the same opinions about movies, she still felt a connection to Britt. "I guess that means you want to continue seeing each other?"

"I can't in good conscience allow you to live your life without savoring the wonder of the greatest movie of all time." Her voice held a hint of sarcasm hidden underneath the outward laugh.

Dana shifted the conversation away from movies. To her surprise, they shared a lot of other interests as well. During the entirety of their two-hour lunch together, she found Britt's politeness and conversation kept her entertained.

By the time there appeared to be a gap in their talk, Dana concluded things were looking up. She could find nothing wrong with Britt. Dana accepted Britt's offer to move their luncheon to her house without hesitation. She wasn't expecting anything to happen, but she imagined herself with Britt on the sofa, cuddling up for the movie, and perhaps sharing a kiss.

They departed in their own automobiles. Dana followed Britt to her apartment, where she parked and entered behind her. As soon as Britt closed the door, darkness descended upon the room. The blackout drapes placed across the windows effectively blocked the light. Dana's astonishment grew when Britt turned on the overhead lights. A large television screen filled an entire wall. Two leather recliners and a small coffee table sat in the center of the room.

So much for cuddling on a sofa, Dana thought, but she said, "That's a serious television."

"I do a lot of serious movie watching. It's my job," Britt said, motioning Dana to follow her down the hall.

Dana stopped when Britt reached for the doorknob, thinking it was a little early to be heading to a bedroom. People moved much faster than in the past, so after a rapid evaluation of the circumstances, Dana conceded to tickling her fancy with Britt. She puffed her chest and pushed forward to the bedroom when Britt opened the door. However, she stopped in the middle of her step when the door opened to a library of movies.

Shelves loaded with DVD and Blu-ray cases. The longest wall in the room had a row of square shelves with what appeared to be records. A few VHS tapes lined the corner. Certainly, a museum of film artifacts.

Britt asked, "Do you have a format preference?"

"What formats?" Dana's face furrowed in puzzlement.

"How would you like to watch Jaws? Blu-ray or Laserdisc? I haven't jumped on the 4K craze because, well, why repurchase films I already own?"

Dana's face contorted with a slow and dramatic nod. "Are these all films? What exactly is a laserdisc?"

Britt walked Dana over to the rack of twelve-inch movie covers and pulled one down to show her the enormous CD-style disc it held. "This is a movie, like a DVD, but bigger. Better quality. More realistic."

Perhaps at the risk of appearing ignorant, Dana shrugged. "Well then, if it's more realistic and you have the movie, we can go with that one. I mean, it really makes no difference to me."

Dana ignored the irritated grunt Britt may or may not have been trying to cover up. Britt lifted the enormous square cover for the movie *Jaws*, then headed out of the room. She remained silent during the entire process. As Britt turned off the lights, Dana quickly followed behind. Britt fiddled with the electronics while Dana wandered around the room, looking at the little movie trinkets. Dana recognized a few characters, like Freddy Krueger and a gorilla from *Planet of the Apes*.

"Please have a seat. What would you want to

drink? A beer? Perhaps a glass of wine?" Britt said to Dana from behind.

She turned around to see Britt standing close. "Water is good," remarked Dana with a grin.

After leaving the room, she returned with a glass of water and a can of soda for herself. Britt signaled for Dana to sit down with a wave of her hand. Dana obliged by taking a seat in a recliner. Britt grabbed the second one as soon as she hit a button on the remote control. Dana gave a quick peek upward at the lights and watched as they gradually dimmed around her while the movie started on the enormous screen mounted on the wall.

Dana attempted to speak during the two-hour film by asking questions about the film, the actors, or simply mentioning something. Britt hushed her each time and never responded to her questions. Dana eventually learned Britt hated talking during the film and kept her mouth shut for the rest of the movie.

Britt turned to Dana as soon as the film concluded and the credits rolled and asked, "What did you think?"

Again, Dana shrugged. "It was okay. But at least I can now say I've seen it."

The sight of Britt leaping from her chair with her hands on her hips astonished Dana. "Okay? Just, okay?"

Dana sank into the chair with a slouch, narrowed her eyes, and murmured, "Um. Sorry. It's just a movie."

If Britt's query surprised her, the subsequent statement undoubtedly took Dana off guard. Britt pressed the button on the remote, which brightened the room, and stated, "I believe you should leave."

Dana sprung from her seat, bewildered beyond belief. "Are you serious?"

"Yeah. You should go. I don't think we're compatible at all."

"Really? Over a movie?"

"*Jaws* is not just a movie. It is a cinematic work of art."

Dana bowed her head and stared at the matted brown carpet below her feet as she searched for the right words to say. The only thing that came to mind was to call this woman out for being a snob over a movie, of all things. Dana finally threw up her hands and acknowledged, "You're absolutely right. I'm going to go. Nice to meet you!"

After saying that, Dana flung open the front door, then slammed it shut behind her. She took a deep breath outside of the apartment and let it out with a guffaw. As she looked up at the blue sky, she pressed her lips together in a straight line and thanked the heavens as she dodged another bullet. No matter how much she liked Britt, they wouldn't be able to have a healthy relationship if they couldn't have disagreements in their perspectives.

Dana ran away as quickly as she could go. The weight of her annoyances pressed heavily on her foot, prompting her to speed down the road at a breakneck pace. She eased off the throttle and calmed her anxieties when she saw her car passing others as if they were standing still. After she collected herself sufficiently, she called Michelle, using the phone on her dashboard. When Michelle answered her phone, she couldn't help but regard a billboard in the distance. On the enormous display, Universal Studios marketed several attractions from the park's history, including the *Jaws* ride as one of them.

"Have you seen the movie *Jaws*?" Dana asked without even extending a greeting.

Michelle stuttered while speaking. "Uh, yeah? Why do you ask?"

"Do you think it's good?"

"Great. Again, why are you asking me this?"

"Would you dump someone if they didn't care for the movie?"

"No." That triggered Michelle's memory. "Wait, didn't you have a date today? Wait! Did she break up with you because of *Jaws*?"

Dana made a bell ringing sound and shouted, "Bingo! Yup. She kicked me out of her house because I didn't enjoy a movie she considered being God's gift to cinema."

Michelle chuckled. "To be fair, it's a really wonderful movie."

"Not you too? Are you breaking up with me now?"

"Well—" Michelle paused jokingly for a moment before continuing. "Wow. Okay. So, who's the next victim on the list?"

Dana arrived at Michelle's residence, exited the vehicle, and knocked on the door. As soon as Michelle opened the front door, Dana dropped the phone from her ear and said, "You really can't expect me to continue this never-ending parade of crackpots."

Michelle opened the front door for Dana and welcomed her inside. "Excluding the film issue, was she that awful? You ended up at her place. How did that happen?"

Dana sat down on the plush sofa, and when Michelle handed her a glass of red wine, she recounted the events of her outing with Britt.

# STELLA

*Hello, I am Stella, and I consider myself a foodie. I have a passion for exploring new restaurants and culinary styles. Let's have dinner together and talk about things.*

After two dates, it was impossible for her to unequivocally assert the dating app was terrible. To a greater extent, it was a source of amusement for her. Reading the profiles was more entertaining than searching the internet for cat memes she could post on Michelle's social media sites. She couldn't respectfully share some profile gems she discovered, but she got a few belly laughs from them.

She engaged in conversation with a few different women in the evenings. After only a few minutes of talking, many of them quickly lost interest. One woman seemed like a therapist, as she continually questioned Dana's feelings about various topics. The persistent way she wanted Dana to discuss *how things made her feel* was a source of angst for her, though she never told the woman how the question made her feel.

There were also an excessive number of persons looking for casual relationships or even couples looking for a third member. On her search for love, she found that no matter how well educated she was, certain terms, such as unicorns and toaster ovens, took on entirely new connotations. That meant she needed to brush up on her urban vocabulary.

Another thing she picked up on was the fact that most of the people who messaged her weren't truly compatible. There wasn't an algorithm doing the work. The computer dumped everyone on her lap, and it was up to her to sift through the crap, hoping to find one good nugget. She found more success with the women she messaged than with the ones who messaged her. It had to be the profile.

Since Dana did not have any unfinished chats, she spent the night swiping left on the unsuitable matches until she found someone who caught her eye. Stella. A woman of fifty-one who lived in the northern part of the city. According to the images, she might have two children, but Dana didn't care either way. She slid her finger to the right on Stella's profile, which loaded the messaging section of the app.

*Food sounds great. Hi. I'm Dana.*

She hated being the one to initiate a conversation. Her messages consistently sounded like the desperation of a lonely lady. If Dana did sound desperate or lonely, Stella did not care. Dana received a reply. They continued a conversation, mostly about food, which was a topic very familiar to Dana.

Dana was one of those people who enjoyed a

delicious meal, even if she never considered herself a foodie. Although Dana enjoyed cooking very much, Bridgette preferred to eat out rather than prepare meals at home. During their time together, they squandered a significant amount of money on food.

After some discussion and back and forth, they agreed on meeting for dinner together the following weekend. There was a brand-new Mexican restaurant which recently opened, and Stella had her heart set on checking it out. That pleased Dana. She could always go for some tacos.

When the day finally arrived, Dana sent a message to Stella just to make sure they were still planning to get together later that evening, after she had closed the shop for the day. They had planned to get together that evening at six o'clock, but Stella mentioned she arrived earlier than expected and already ordered a margarita at the bar. Dana thought it was a wonderful idea, so she headed in that direction. When Dana arrived, Stella hadn't had just one margarita. She estimated Stella had at least three or four drinks, based on her appearance.

Dana waved to the bartender and ordered a peach margarita on the rocks. Stella yelled, "Put it on my tab."

"Thanks." Stella's offer was really kind and thoughtful. Dana was not the type of person to let other people to pay for her. Even when Dana's friends wound up paying, she always paid them back. Being the first date, Dana allowed Stella to treat her to a drink, but she'd pay for the food, or at least her portion of it.

Stella suggested, "Since you're here, why don't we get a table and start eating?"

"I don't mind sitting at the bar for a little while. We're nearly an hour earlier than expected, and I am not very hungry; unless you are?"

Stella may not have shown her irritation verbally, but it was clear from the look on her face she would have preferred to be getting on with the portion of their evening that involved eating. "Okay, sure. We can hang out here."

Dana hiked herself onto the barstool next to Stella so she could strike up a conversation while assessing her. Stella's profile photos hid nothing. She provided everyone a look at her world, including a full-body photo of herself taken at what appeared to be an outdoor celebration. A lot of users only posted the most flattering of images. Maybe that was what attracted Dana to Stella. She was real. Even though Stella was heavier than Dana's ideal woman, she was still quite attractive. Sitting so close, Dana fully appreciated the woman's flawless skin and exquisite features.

Just as Dana was ready to ask about Stella's day, Stella peered at her and remarked, "I pictured you to be larger based on your comments about enjoying food so much."

Dana shifted the conversation after being taken aback by her statement. Were they were already talking weight this early in their relationship? "When I can, I do my best to get outside, and I eat fairly healthily at home."

Stella reached out and lightly pinched Dana's hip. "No. It's okay. I just assumed you'd be heavier. I was slightly concerned for a moment, but you're all right."

Though Dana placed little importance on her size, she found it odd that the remarks came from a woman twice her size. Given the way the date began, Dana did not have high hopes for a romantic match.

After they drained a round of margaritas, they shuffled to the table for a meal together. Dana crammed herself into the booth while giving the table a slight nudge for a bit more room on her side.

Stella noticed. "Do you need some extra space?" As Stella pulled the table away with another quip, Dana's gaze shot upward. "There. Now you'll fit."

In Dana's experience, politeness usually prevailed. As she took her seat in the booth, a false grin spread across her face. There was no justification for causing a commotion. "Thank you."

When the waiter arrived at the table with a basket of chips and a bowl of salsa, Stella prevented the gentleman from leaving until she sampled them. She hummed her approval after the first dip. "Bring out another basket and salsa for her."

Dana waved at her disagreement. "No. It's unnecessary. I'm fine."

"You sure?" Stella asked.

"Positive."

"Just another bowl of salsa then." Stella said to the waiter, awaiting instruction. Stella scooped up more salsa onto the same chip and popped it into her mouth. She made a gesture toward Dana. "Have some. It's fantastic salsa."

Dana passed. "I will in a bit."

"Are you upset I called you fat?" Stella asked.

The question took Dana aback, perhaps even more so than before. They returned to the topic after assuming they'd moved on. Dana's blood pressure increased as she studied Stella's facial expression, obviously concerned about her weight. She made a beeline for the glass of water, drained it in one swift motion, and sat it back down. "I don't necessarily think you called me fat."

"I did." Stella supplied no further information other than to confirm she, indeed, called her fat.

She drew her first word out of her mouth. "Okay. Are you trying to provoke me or instigate a fight?"

"No. I'm just puzzled as to why I didn't offend you when I called you fat."

"I'd prefer you stop using the word fat, but I see no need to argue."

Stella nodded. "Because rather than discussing, you'll simply ghost me after this date."

Dana continued to smile, as phony as it was, and said, "This is not off to a good start. Perhaps we should start over, or have I offended you in some way?"

"No. Not at all. I'm simply testing the waters. You passed, sort of."

Dana's eyes widened in bewilderment. "Passed what? A test?"

"Yes. Everywhere I travel, I am criticized for being overweight. Many times a day, I hear snarky comments about it. Someone just called you out on your weight, but you didn't react negatively. You don't care what others think?"

Dana jumped in. "I don't. I'm content with who I am."

"Great. This bodes well for us because I am, too."

Dana nodded, keeping her uneasiness. "But you said sort of, so that means you don't really believe I passed whatever test you are giving me."

"You didn't get angry or call me out on my bullshit. This means you are passive, and you let others to get away with their negativity, thus enabling social discrimination."

Dana did not like being put to the test. She would likely tell Stella things didn't work out, but she would never ghost her. "I believe it's not worth the effort. I can only change how it affects me; you cannot change other people. The fact you manipulated my responses on a test I ultimately failed should make me pretty angry. Instead, I recognize this isn't an ideal approach to a possible future relationship."

Stella chuckled and grinned. She took another chip from the basket and scooped more salsa into her mouth. Stella remarked with a full mouth, "Oh, honey. Yeah. We certainly aren't compatible. I could have told you that from your profile."

She almost choked on her drink as her surprise at Stella's statements caused her to spit out a little. "Why the hell did you agree to go on a date with me?"

"For dinner. You invited me to dinner. I'm not going to turn down a free meal."

*Wow.* "Wow!" Dana let out a roaring laugh from deep within. Dana's smile even took Stella aback with a shocked expression. "You must be the most fascinating person I've ever met. Seriously. I cannot believe you only agreed to meet because I'd buy you dinner. Moreover, you told me that was the sole reason you came out. Stella, you are a work of art."

Stella replied, "I believe in honesty."

The waitress approached the table. "Are you both ready to order?"

Dana spoke before Stella responded. "I admire your convictions, so go ahead. I'll buy you dinner, Stella."

Stella ordered. Thankfully, not the entire menu. When the server glanced at Dana for her order, she declined and took out her credit card. "Charge it on the credit card. I won't be staying."

"What? No dinner."

"Stella, I respect your authenticity, but I'd rather have dinner with someone who values me and my company more than the food I'm buying. I hope you find what you're looking for on the Internet."

The server returned with the bill and card. Dana signed the paper, tucked her card into her purse, and left the booth quickly. "Thank you, Stella, for an enlightening evening."

And Dana made her way out of the restaurant. It wasn't a huge amount of money to throw away. She had done considerably worse in splurging for other people, such as women who joined Bridgette for dinner and presumably had her wife for dessert. Dana eventually concluded her experiences were just that. Experiences. In the future, she would become more adept at reading people's intentions.

On her way home, Dana stopped at a quaint café which she particularly enjoyed. Even though it wasn't tacos, her BLT sandwich with a homemade pickle was delicious. She browsed the news website in peace while she savored her meal alone. The top two articles were about recent killings in the city, which prompted her to be concerned about how deadly the city had become in recent years. The distant sound of a police siren ignited the thought of the lone member of the police force she recognized by name. Morales. The warmth of Dana's heart shone through in her smile. *Stay safe, Morales.*

# CYPRUS

*Hi. I'm Cyprus. Love, aesthetics, and procreation are the qualities I most strongly identify with my own life. I'm a very passionate person who loves love. Beautiful animals make me happy. Women who make my life brighter are welcome.*

For a few weeks, Dana did not open the dating app. She wasn't ready to tackle all the alerts of interested possibilities. After feeling dejected by a woman whose only interest was in receiving a free meal, Dana didn't want to continue on her quest for love. Michelle and Scott both encouraged her to keep going and not let work be an excuse, which stopped her from going out.

Dana, with Mr. Jinx in her lap and a cup of coffee at her side, pulled out her phone and launched the app so she could laugh at the overwhelming number of likes she'd received. She found it odd her profile was getting so many views, yet she hadn't come across too many people that piqued her interest. Perhaps she set the bar too high. For some reason, she swiped left more times than swiping right.

Her finger rode on autopilot as she repeatedly flipped through pages of people whose faces didn't interest her. As she prepared to swipe again, a lovely face drew her attention. She kept her finger on the screen as she scrolled upward to read the profile.

There wasn't a lot of information provided in the three-hundred character description, but the images showed a gorgeous woman sniffing flowers in the wide field. Dana started a chat log with Cyprus by swiping right on the screen and sending her a message with the flick of her finger.

*Hello and happy Saturday to you. I hope everything is going well for you. If you're interested in talking, let me know. Profiles do not paint a full picture of a person. I'd like to learn more about you.*

Even though it seemed quite basic, Dana drew a blank when it came to striking up a positive conversation. Since the app showed Cyprus online, Dana browsed a couple of messages she received while she waited for Cyprus to answer. She responded to several messages, only to see if the leads led to anything intriguing. Dana threw her phone on the sofa in a huff when one of them responded with a message asking for her address so they could have an early roll in the sheets. She cringed at the thought of random sex hook-ups.

By the middle of the afternoon, Dana still hadn't heard from Cyprus, so she reasoned the woman must not be interested. Not receiving a reply was not unexpected. She sent messages to other profiles in the past that interested her but received no responses. Before Dana could update her profile, an alert flashed across the screen with Cyprus's name.

*Sorry for the delay in responding; life just wasn't on my side this morning. Everything is OK now, and I can concentrate on something else, such as you. Hi. Do you want to meet some place for coffee? If you don't like coffee, how about ice cream?*

The message was a little too forward for her liking, since it was presumptuous Dana wanted to meet so quickly. Dana responded. *Do people just throw caution to the wind and meet up with a stranger without truly getting to know one another? Maybe I'm far too old school for this, but is this something people do?*

After waiting for a while, Dana finally got an answer, but it was not what she expected. *I believe in personal interaction rather than hiding behind words on a screen, but that's just me.*

That's the kind of answer Dana liked to hear. Human relationships. It's possible she had an inaccurate impression of the dating app. The only way to form a human connection with another person was to physically interact with them and gauge how the energy made her feel. After saying that, Dana suggested a charming coffee shop close to her house and promised to meet Cyprus later that day.

A woman entered the coffee shop dressed head to toe in dark clothing, including a black shawl she wore over her shoulders. Dana rose to welcome the strangely clothed woman, since she had a familiar face. "Cyprus?" questioned Dana as she extended her hand.

The lady gave Dana's hand a shake. "Yes. Hi, Dana. I'm delighted you agreed to meet. I despise all this technology, including dating apps, but it's a necessary evil since people today choose to isolate themselves. Everything is now being delivered, and no one leaves their residences."

Hearing someone else had the same feelings Dana had regarding this new means of finding potential life partners was like a breath of fresh air. They approached the counter. Dana asked for a tall mocha white latte. When Cyprus ordered the same drink, they instantly connected.

As they sat down at the booth with their beverages, Dana picked up where Cyprus left off. "I concur wholeheartedly with your assessment of phone-based dating. It's refreshing to find someone who agrees. The main reason I was apprehensive to meet in person was because it seems like if someone is ready to meet, they want only one thing."

Cyprus wrapped her black shawl even more snugly over her shoulders, as though she tried to conceal her figure. Dana considered it peculiar, particularly considering the temperature had already reached ninety degrees outdoors.

Cyprus said, "Sex," with a further pull on her shawl. "Yes. Yes. And although I understand the human yearning for this act, it is not one to be taken lightly."

Dana took a drink of her coffee and smiled

politely at the lady sitting across the table from her, someone she knew very little about. As Cyprus continued to talk, Dana's curiosity rose exponentially; quite satisfied the subject rapidly shifted away from sex to more engaging issues, like as spirituality and enlightenment. Cyprus had an air of calmness Dana found to be invigorating, which contributed to the easygoing and relaxed vibe that pervaded their interaction.

Dana found she could have an intellectual conversation with Cyprus. They didn't talk about anything personal, like relationships or other common topics like family or hobbies. Much more enjoyable than either of her previous three dates, but there was still something a little off about the way Cyprus incessantly held her shawl close to her body.

After an hour or so of conversation, Dana asked, "Are you cold or uncomfortable?"

"No. Why do you ask?" Cyprus replied.

"You keep pulling your sweater up. Is there a breeze there? If you are cold, we can move or go outside."

Cyprus waved her hands around, trying to dispel Dana's concern. "Oh, no. The temperature is comfortable. Knowing the strength of my aura makes me extremely cautious around others."

The comment caused Dana's head to tilt to the side while her eyes narrowed and eyebrows raised. "You are going to have to explain that to me. I have no idea what that means."

She once more brought her shawl to her neck. "No

worries, my dear. My cloak protects others from the spiritual deities that inhabit my body. If I exposed you to my abilities, you might not be able to resist the urge to sleep with me tonight. I will not unleash this power until I am certain you are deserving of the amount of fervor the gods have granted me."

Dana puckered her lips and bobbed her head up and down while suppressing a laugh. "Are you saying I wouldn't be able to control myself if I saw you naked?"

"Dana, you are too precious for that now. I must really protect you because sleeping together so soon is detrimental to the soul. We have to wait."

"Although I'm confident I can control myself, you are correct. It's definitely not good for the soul." At that precise moment, Dana resisted the urge to rise to her feet and leave the coffee shop. Once more, another insane person crossed her path, and if that was the type of person her profile attracted, she needed to reevaluate it.

Cyprus extended her hand across the table and grabbed Dana's hand, clenching it in her grip. "You do not fully comprehend my powers. They are significantly greater than your willpower. Although I feel a strong connection with you at the moment, we must wait. Lead us not into temptation—"

Dana withdrew her hand from Cyprus as she listened in shock to the biblical passage being recited to her. As she pushed herself up from the table with an almost dizzying stance, her throat tightened. Dana's eyes blurred as she said, "Well, I'm not going to be in a place where temptation could overwhelm me, so I'm going. Thank you for the pleasant conversation, but I must protect myself."

Dana spun around and marched toward the exit, tossing her cup into the garbage can on the way out of the building. As she pushed through the double doors, the intense heat of Orlando blasted her in the face, and within a split second, beads of sweat formed on the small of her back. As she struggled to rid her body of the eerie energy emanating from Cyprus, the hairs on the back of her neck stood on end.

Dana had time to think while she traveled home. To begin, she needed to make some changes to her profile. The concept of being single and ready to mingle wasn't doing her any favors. There were four dates total, and none of them were successful. So she had a thing for Britt. Britt, on the other hand, concluded it was essential for their preferences in films to coincide.

While thinking of her past failures, Dana did not come to a full and complete stop at the intersection when she turned the corner on a red light. As she looked in the rearview mirror and saw the flashing red lights behind her, the siren jolted her out of her thoughts about crazy women. She exclaimed, "Fuck," as she slowed to a stop.

The police officer approached her vehicle after stepping out of the patrol car. Dana kept both of her hands on the steering wheel in order to comply with the rules. Dana cast a glance in the direction of the police officer when she stopped at the driver's side door. Her gaze ventured upward, but not before she finished reading the name tag, which simply stated Morales. When Dana's eyes landed on the officer's features, a grin broke out on her face.

"The flower shop lady," Morales said, and they both laughed. "I really don't want to give you a ticket."

"Thank you, but I completely understand," Dana said, knowing what she had done wrong. "Let me get my license out of my purse."

Officer Morales dismissed it with a wave of her hand. "Don't worry. Just be sure to stop at these intersections and drive safely. I'm sure someone wants you to come home every day."

"My cat. Sorry about the light, too. Thank you for not ticketing me. I appreciate it."

"You have a good day, flower lady." Morales thumped the car door several times before returning to her vehicle. In her side mirror, Dana checked out Morales and the sway of her hips with each confident stride.

Dana exhaled loudly as Morales slipped into the vehicle behind her. "Why the hell do you have to be a cop?"

Dana turned the key in the ignition and drove off. As the police car followed her, she monitored her rear view. Dana turned onto her street, but the patrol car drove straight ahead. The idea of a sexy cop following her home and performing a strip search ended as quickly as it began.

# ELENA

*Elena. 52. Soft and butch while still being a woman. Looking for same. No drama. No hook-ups.*

**W**hile reading the profile of a woman who had messaged her, Dana felt her breasts. She said aloud, "They are indeed real."

After the last wedding, Miguel left the flower shop early because business had slowed down significantly. It was like being in Death Valley during the summer if there were no floral events. Dana was about to send Elena a message when she heard the cowbell that hung from the front door. She used it to alert the staff to a customer even if they were in the back. She tossed her phone to the side and rounded the corner to greet the client. Dana almost froze in her tracks as the police officer from earlier entered. She continued forward with a genuine smile.

"I told you I'd be here," Officer Morales said as she approached the counter with large, gleaming eyes. "You stopping at those lights?"

"I am. You are a woman of your word." While searching for the memory, Dana pointed at her. "Flower arrangement for your mother? Correct?"

"A woman with memory. Yes. Her birthday is tomorrow. Do you deliver? Please say yes."

When Dana saw the officer's pleading expression, she couldn't help but crack a grin. If she had more courage, she would reach across the counter and grab the officer by the bulletproof vest for a passionate kiss. No need to be arrested for assault of a peace officer. Dana's demeanor remained unruffled as she calmly retrieved an order form from beneath the counter. "Of course. We can arrange for delivery in the morning. Do you know your mother's favorite flower or color?"

"Oh, I'm not really sure. Something pretty." Officer Morales smiled with her eyebrows raised. Surely a flirtatious move. "What would you suggest?"

Dana pushed herself forward and arched her back while drawing her feminine side out from within. Her tone became more soothing, as if talking about flowers were a stimulating conversation starter. "This time of year, everyone enjoys sunflowers because it is summer. Maybe a few roses added. We just received a shipment of exquisite antique heirloom carnations."

"Sounds perfect."

At precisely the same moment Officer Morales appeared to suggest something else, Michelle and Scott walked through the front door of the shop, laughing at a joke they just shared with each other. Michelle raised her hand when she noticed the customer. "Oops. Sorry. We'll behave."

Dana's two best friends continued their conversation as they walked past the counter and into the back. They discussed getting together for a few drinks after work, but their unexpected visit took Dana aback. As Dana cast a glance over her shoulder toward her companions, the officer took a few steps back and to the side. It appeared as though the connection or previous spark fizzled. Sometimes she disliked when they acted like they owned the store when they came in.

She pushed the order form across the counter and asked the officer to fill it out with her information and the delivery instructions.

The officer's radio let out a high-pitched screech. Morales lowered the volume and hurriedly filled out the form. A few more words over the radio quickened her pace. "Thank you. I gotta run. I'm certain my mother will enjoy it."

As Morales dashed out the door, Dana gave her a wave. She quickly scanned the paperwork and made a mental note of the officer's name. Cynthia Morales.

"I understand you got preached at by the Goddess of Love," Scott said as Dana returned to the design area of the shop.

"Nowhere near a goddess. More like a cult member. Can I take a break from dating apps?"

Scott and Michelle both simultaneously exclaimed, "No!"

Then Scott inquired, "Do you have any upcoming dates planned?"

"No, although I was about to send a message to

an Elena. She said she wanted a real woman, although I am unsure what this means in modern parlance." Dana entered her office, retrieved her phone, then passed it to her friends over the table.

Michelle picked it up and inspected the profile picture. "A little masculine, but not horrifying. Let's just invite her out."

As Michelle typed, Dana's eyes widened, and heart raced as she watched. "What're you doing?"

Michelle spoke as she typed the words: *Hey. Getting together with some friends at Panda Brewery tonight at 6 p.m. Want to get together? Something casual?*

Michelle pressed the send button, and Dana cringed. "No. Really. Why did you do that?"

"That was absolutely perfect. If you find her interesting, we'll scat. If she's a wench, you have friends who will get rid of her," Scott said.

On the other side of the table from Dana, Scott and Michelle engaged in a back-and-forth conversation about the most recent episodes of the television shows they currently followed. While taking sips of her beer, Dana cast a curious glance at the entrance. As she waited for the door to open, her attention wandered to the bar, where she noted a stunning Latina woman moving her finger along the rim of a beer glass. The woman's long, dark hair did a good job of framing her face. Dana sensed she had seen the woman somewhere before, but she could not place her. She quickly darted her eyes to the door as it opened and glimpsed Elena coming in. Dana beckoned her over to their table with a wave of her hand.

As Elena approached them, Dana scooted in to make room next to her for Elena. Dana introduced her friends, allowing Elena to greet them and tell them about herself. Michelle provided a small amount of unspoken approval with her eyes to Dana. With this laid-back get-together, both of her friends played an active role in breaking the ice and keeping the conversation casual. The more people Dana dated, the more difficult it became for her to find things to talk about, like the tedious game of twenty questions.

Dana didn't understand how to switch gears so effortlessly, unlike Michelle, who mastered it like an art form. She didn't even hear Michelle ask a question, but Dana already knew more about Elena in just a short amount of time. More than she did with any of her other dates.

Scott's focus shifted momentarily as a group of strikingly good-looking men entered the room, almost as if on a timer. He made his excuse and bowed out, presumably on his way to find his next sugar daddy. Immediately after, Michelle got up and went to the bathroom to relieve herself.

Elena tightened her lips and turned to face Dana. "I suppose I passed the test with your friends now that we're alone."

Dana laughed and widened her toothy smile. "Was it that obvious?"

"A little, but I understand completely. Blind dates and meeting new people can be nerve-wracking. You must be shy?" Elena asked.

"I am an introvert, but after a few drinks, I become more extroverted."

Elena pushed Dana's pint of beer toward her with a chuckle. "Let's get you a little more talkative."

Elena's eyes sparkled with a flirtatious look as Dana drank from the glass. With Elena's gleaming smile upon her, Dana felt a strong urge to let her guard down. It would take more than one beer for Dana to break out of her shell, especially considering the growing silence between the two of them. Dana didn't want to start with a bunch of boring questions that led to nowhere, but Elena's alluring stare tightened the growing sexual tension between them.

Dana had to break the silence or else she would go insane. "I own a flower shop."

Clearly surprised, Elena's brow furrowed, and she asked, "A lesbian florist? I was unaware they existed. I thought most florists were straight moms with two-point-five kids who had nothing better to do while their husbands were at work screwing the secretaries."

Dana responded, "Actually, many lesbians and bisexuals are florists. We don't all fit under that same straight umbrella."

"Most bisexual women are not truly bisexual. I mean, the majority of bisexual women are more bi-curious, living in a heteronormative household with the same number of children."

Dana nodded with her head cocked, uncertain of how to respond.

Elena made a hand gesture in the air. "Unless you feel you are bisexual, but I'm sure your profile read lesbian."

"Oh, I am a lesbian, but I am unsure if I concur with your assessment of bisexual women."

"We can agree to disagree. I'd rather not argue on the first date, especially since I want to learn more about you."

She gave in and agreed to change the subject, agreeing to keep the tone of the conversation very light. When Dana finished another full two beers, both guards were down and laughter ensued. Even Dana's more feminine side manifested itself during the date, as evident by her high-pitched giggles and the increased ease with which her hands touched Elena.

As soon as Elena slipped away to the restroom, Michelle made her way over to the booth to check in with Dana. After a brief exchange only lasting a few seconds, Michelle decided it was time to call it a night before Elena came back. They parted ways and made plans to talk first thing in the morning.

When Elena returned to the table, she slid in next to Dana and put a glass of water in front of her. Elena could have sat across from her since her friends wouldn't be returning, but she chose not to. There was most certainly a connection. Dana didn't mind the increased proximity at all.

Elena pushed the water toward Dana, bribing her to drink. "I don't want you even slightly intoxicated when you drive home tonight, so drink up!"

Dana assured her, "I'm not drunk."

"Still. I'd like to see you again after tonight if you're up to it. So, drink."

Dana drained the water from the glass. As she replaced the glass on the table, the realization she consumed an excessive amount of alcohol struck her. It was imperative she eat something before getting behind the wheel. "Two doors down is a diner. Want to go? I'm a tad hungry and can use something to soak up the alcohol."

"It will take more than a small amount of food to sober you up. I should drive you home or call an Uber for you. Unless your friends come back?"

Dana grinned. "I'd let you take me home."

"Well, okay." Elena slid out of the booth and aided Dana in standing.

Dana pointed to the back of the bar. "I need to pee first."

Elena held Dana steady as she walked to the bathroom. While sitting in the stall and forcing herself to urinate, Dana overheard Elena say, "This is the women's restroom."

"I'm a woman," responded a deep, husky voice. "I'm transitioning."

"If you have a penis, you're a male. You need to leave."

Dana pressed her lips together, listening as to what was being said.

"I have the right to be in this restroom," the deepened voice repeated. "I'm just as much a woman as you."

"Again, God gave you a penis. God gave you a man's intellect, testosterone, and desires. Now, leave before I make a scene."

She squeaked out a tiny stream of urine. Dana had trouble using the restroom in the presence of other people. With two others, she couldn't make a sound. She heaved a sigh and took a deep breath as she heard the door to the restroom open and close. After looking under the stall, Dana did not find any feet. Her bladder finally emptied, expelling all the liquid in her body.

It would have taken a lot more beer for her to have failed to comprehend the conversation and argument that transpired while she waited for privacy. As she left the bathroom, she saw Elena blocking the bathroom from a person who clearly needed to use it.

Dana drew Elena away from the entrance with a strong tug. "C'mon, now. There's no reason for us to gate keep a bathroom."

This remark appeared to anger Elena as she yanked her arm away from Dana. "Gatekeeping? Really? I have serious issues with men entering women's restrooms under the guise of being female. It is merely an excuse to prey on vulnerable women, especially in bars where most women are under the influence."

Dana's voice grew louder. "I am not drunk enough to be vulnerable to someone trying to take a piss. Man. Woman. Who gives a damn?"

"You will if an individual who claims to be taking estrogen rapes you. If he were a woman, he would wear a dress rather than jeans like his buddies."

A disagreement arose out of this situation because Dana refused to back down. She faced Elena. "Then why are you not wearing a dress? Who gave you the authority to choose who is transgender and who is not? I'm fairly certain there are lesbian women in the world who also prey on drunk, defenseless girls. You dislike bisexuals, and now transwomen who are just trying to use the stinkin' bathroom. I'm pretty sure, at this point, I don't want you to take me home."

As soon as the speech ended, everyone in the bar started clapping. No words came out of Elena's mouth as she pushed her way past Dana, knocking shoulders with her as she went.

As the applause subsided, she nodded and stated aloud, "Now I'm going to need a ride home because I'm too drunk to drive."

When the Latin woman at the counter slid off her barstool, it was a split second too late. By the time she ended up a few steps away from Dana, Scott already pounced on her like any good best friend. "Come on, you little spokesperson for all of us social misfits. I'll drive your inebriated little ass home. You'll have to pay me back for this, since Scottie won't get any tonight."

The mysterious woman said in a raspy voice, just as Scott placed his hand under Dana's arm. "You know, I certainly don't mind giving her a ride."

Scott declined the offer. "Thank you, sweetie, but I can't just give my friend to anyone. No offense. I mean, you seem nice and everything."

Dana peered with squinted eyes at the woman,

whose voice rang in her ears like wedding bells. The beer hit her hard. She smiled at them and mumbled incoherently, "I like you. I like her, Scott."

"Baby girl, when you're drunk, you like everyone. This is why I am driving you home." Scott twirled Dana toward the exit, carried her out to his car, then drove Dana home so that she could sleep off the effects of the excess alcohol.

# TIFFANY

*Isn't it great to date online? Even though it can be hard sometimes, it's still fun to have the chance to meet someone special who you might not have met otherwise. Also, my name is Tiffany.*

Dana hadn't used the dating app for close to three months, and from the very beginning, she had nothing but terrible dates. Even though she argued with her closest friends about how she needed to disconnect herself from it, she had not done so. Getting up every morning and reading all the messages from potential suitors became ritualistic, and she found it quite addicting. She messaged a few people here and there, keeping some conversations longer than others. Even though Scott had instructed her to ignore people she found uninteresting, she still sent them messages, wishing them well and saying goodbye.

She didn't like it when people disappeared without a trace. It seemed impolite to ignore someone when they continued to send messages. Even though it hadn't happened to her, the more people she messaged, the greater the likelihood that it would happen. The odds were not in her favor.

Tiffany, the woman with whom Dana corresponded with over the past few days, messaged Dana that morning with some quite surprising information. Tiffany made it a habit to stop by a bar on her way home from work. The same bar Dana often hung out with Michelle and Scott. Dana became transfixed on Tiffany's photograph as she deliberated over the possibility she had met the woman at some point in the past. She couldn't place her. Then again, Dana rarely paid attention to anyone but themselves.

It was a Wednesday, which meant drinks at the bar were fifty percent off, so Dana asked Tiffany to meet up after work for a few drinks. Tiffany agreed.

When Dana closed the shop for the day, she brushed her hair in the bathroom mirror and inspected her wardrobe. After she realized the glitter she worked with earlier in the day had made its way onto her shirt, she probably should have not asked someone out on a date. She dusted it off and shrugged. A day in the life of a florist. It's just a fact of life: glitter found its way into the strangest nooks and crannies.

When Dana arrived at the bar, she greeted the extremely hot and very straight bartender with a wave, then glanced around to find Tiffany. Because of her dark, curly hair, she shouldn't be too difficult to recognize. Even if pulled back, the hair would give her away.

The bartender leaned over the bar and hollered at Dana. "You looking for someone?"

The thick Latin accent of the bartender was one of Dana's favorite things about the woman, and if she weren't the most straight woman in the world, Dana would have asked her out. She retrieved her phone from her purse and flashed a picture of Tiffany in front of her. "Have you seen her?"

"Yeah. Tiff. She's in the back. Probably playing pool."

Dana wrinkled her brow in confusion as she peered toward the far end of the bar. She did not know that the establishment even housed pool tables. Dana nodded and shuffled her way to the back, where she ducked around a corner and into a completely unfamiliar area. The expansive room contained four pool tables and a couple of dart boards.

Dana grinned as she thought about the newly discovered forms of entertainment she could take part in. She had done nothing besides take a booth and use the restroom at the opposite end of the pub.

After sinking a ball in the side pocket, Tiffany lifted from the table and cast a glance in Dana's direction. She drank from the beer bottle sitting on the edge of the table and rocked toward Dana, who approached the table. Tiffany was taller than Dana by one full head. Her posture was upright, tall, and self-assured; she exuded a sense of femininity, especially when she smiled. "Hi. You must be Dana. I'm Tiffany. You can call me Tiff."

As she greeted Dana, the light from the room

glistened in her eyes, creating a twinkling effect. Dana tilted her head back in order to meet Tiffany's gaze. She became conscious of how it must have appeared to the people around her as she gazed with a warm smile. Instead of losing herself in Tiffany's eyes, Dana diverted her attention elsewhere as she greeted her. "Nice to meet you, Tiff."

Tiffany led Dana to the pool table, where a second woman awaited her return. Since she put a solid into the corner pocket, it was still her turn. "This is Steph, my cousin. She's waiting for her husband to get off work, but if her presence bothers you, she'll make herself scarce."

Dana offered her hand to Steph. At least Tiffany did her best to avoid any awkward situations by explaining the woman's presence right from the start. "No. Not at all. Hi. I'm Dana."

When Tiffany leaned over the table and aimed at the balls, Dana's vantage point allowed her to take in Tiffany's strong feminine confidence. Dana's chest tightened as she took in the beautiful scenery. Although she was single, she was still alive and found pleasure in the company of attractive women. Tiffany certainly fit the bill.

After Tiffany's shot was unsuccessful, she sat down on the stool next to Dana and gave Steph the opportunity to play. Dana centered her attention on Tiffany and examined her thoroughly, beginning with her hair and ending with her shoes. The way Tiffany leaned back caused a tug on her white button-down dress shirt, which emphasized the firmness of her breasts.

Dana's eyes darted all around the room to avoid being noticed for staring too long. "I did not know there were pool tables in the back. I've been coming here for several years without knowing."

Tiffany took a sip of her beer and said, "Perhaps that's why we've never seen each other before."

"Probably, but I am sure I would have noticed you," Dana mentioned, then her face flushed and sweat beaded on her back as she stutteringly retracted her embarrassing statement. "I mean, seen you. Typically, I am up front with my friends. Not paying much attention to this area, to be honest."

Tiffany reached out and fingered Dana's hand. "You're cute. I understood what you meant. "

Dana stated, not wanting Tiffany to feel her clammy hands, "I'm just a little nervous. Sorry. I just can't seem to master the art of dating. Everything seems so in your face."

She stood and crossed in front of Dana to take her turn. Tiffany leaned over the table as she shot the cue and said, "You need to relax. Have you been to a strip club before?"

The question stunned Dana, causing her to nearly choke on her own saliva. "Um. No. I've been in a relationship for over twenty years, so I had no need for that."

Tiffany laughed as her shot missed the shot. "There's nothing inherently wrong with that. Many couples enjoy watching their partner get turned on by another person. Reduces monotony."

"We didn't have that issue." Dana reassured her and herself that their sexual life was enjoyable. "Our sex life was fine. Hot. I mean, it wasn't boring."

Tiffany approached Dana and whispered in her ear with an air of superiority. "I'm sure it was hot." She pulled away and said as casually as possible, "Before you asked me out tonight, I had plans to go to a club. Why don't you join me? It will be entertaining, and I'll pop your stripper cherry."

Through the entirety of their conversation, the woman could not help but laugh at Dana's timidity. Dana did not want to be considered a prude, so she thought to herself, "What the hell?"

As Dana walked into the strip club, following one step behind Tiffany, her eyes quickly adjusted to the dim lighting of the establishment. Tiffany paid the cover, then led Dana with her hand on the small of her back; a romantic gesture that linked them as a couple to those who noted their presence.

Having someone in her life as stunningly beautiful as Tiffany brought to mind Bridgette, who exuded an aura of confidence and radiance at all times. She was the center of everyone's attention whenever they turned their heads in her direction. Dana felt a wave of uncertainty wash over her as she saw her reflection alongside Tiffany on the mirrored wall. Even though Dana was not short, compared to Tiffany, she appeared to be quite small, stocky, and uninteresting. In the same fashion as when she walked alongside Bridgette.

They navigated their way through the enticing music and the pulsating lights. A woman with nothing covering her chest swayed to the music while wearing only the bottom of her bikini, hoping to get some singles from some horny and eager men.

Dana scanned the room, searching for other women among the patrons, but found none. She leaned toward Tiffany as the two walked in step. "Are women even allowed in here?"

Tiffany draped her arm across Dana's shoulder and drew her in close. "Of course. We're like royalty because we're safe."

Dana didn't know what that meant, but she went along with Tiffany as they found a couple of comfortable chairs a few feet from the stage. After they took their seats, a hostess welcomed them and took their drink orders.

When they were once again alone, Tiffany asked, "So, what's your poison?"

"Excuse me?" Dana asked while hovering over the table to hear her over the music.

"Poison. Chicks. What's your type?"

Dana had given little thought to her ideal partner beyond her ex-wife. Even when she browsed the profiles at random on the app, identifying a pattern of what she liked or disliked in a potential partner was far from her mind. Dana shrugged with her lips pursed inward. "I don't think I have one. I'm kind of all over the place."

Tiffany responded, "I don't believe it. Everyone has a preference or a type."

Dana argued in favor of her position. "It's the person who I like, not their appearance." After she said that, she realized that wasn't always the case. Because she was more of a tomboy, she yearned for a more feminine partner and consequently avoided butches. They were at a strip club; it didn't matter. Most of the dancers were feminine and stunningly attractive.

When Tiffany refused to back down, Dana shook her head and said, "Okay. Blonde, or blondish."

Tiffany's grin grew wider and wider. "A woman after my own heart. I believe we're going to get along just fine."

Dana wasn't blonde. Although neither was Tiffany, they shared a preference for blonde-haired women. *How could they possibly get along, as Tiffany stated?*

Tiffany motioned the hostess to come over, then whispered something in her ear. The hostess excused herself. Shortly thereafter, a voluptuous blonde with ample breasts took her place. As she spoke, she leaned over the table. Neither of her breasts moved nor drooped in a downward direction. She said, "Twenty for three minutes. Fifty for a private room."

Dana stared at Tiffany blankly. It was Tiffany's idea to invite this woman over, but she did not reach for her wallet. Preferring to dismiss this woman instead of paying, Dana reluctantly pulled out a twenty from her wallet and handed it to the woman.

Tiffany wiggled in her seat, much like a kid in a candy store. She shifted for a better view of the blonde stripper, placing the bill in her bikini, then sitting on Dana's lap. The woman nestled her butt cheeks in Dana's lap as she gyrated her body. A look of embarrassment spread across Dana's face. It felt like the longest three minutes of Dana's life, especially since the woman who enjoyed it most wasn't the one receiving the lap dance. Dana's nervousness shook her core and an uncontrollable hum of spasms spread throughout her whole body. It wasn't because Dana got off to the woman on her lap; the idea of Tiffany's own excitement over it filled her with awkward disgust.

After the three minutes, the stripper licked Dana's lips and rose from Dana's lap. Tiffany leaned to Dana and said in an airy tone, "God, I want to fuck you so much right now!"

Dana surprised herself by turning her head and darting her eyes toward Tiffany. "Yeah, that's not happening."

Tiffany responded with an identical expression of shock. "Seriously? You're not the least bit turned on by that?"

Dana's irate tone tore through the music beats. "Even if I were, I'd rather be with her than with the woman who masturbated to it."

"I didn't masturbate."

"I'm pretty sure you wanted to."

"That's the whole point of strip clubs."

"Perhaps this explains why I'd never come here."

"So, you're really not in the mood?"

"I'm not now." That was a lie. Dana experienced a tingling sensation in the space between her thighs.

More so from their petty argument than from the stripper. Much like with Bridgette, it typically culminated in the two of them having heated hate sex. However, Dana was not the type of person to initiate the arguments that ultimately led to great sex. She definitely wouldn't stop Tiffany if their argument took over the situation.

Tiffany instead rose from her chair in a huff. "Wow. And I truly had high expectations for you." She handed the same blonde a bill, then the two of them walked hand in hand behind a curtain at the back of the bar.

Dana snorted, taking a deep breath of stale, smokey air after being abandoned. After paying the bill, she made her way out of the club. She leaned against her car in the parking lot and considered going back inside to meet with Tiffany behind a curtain. Ultimately, she decided not to do so because the similarities between Tiffany and Bridgette were uncanny. Even Michelle would have agreed with that assessment. With that reason, Dana ducked into her car and fled as soon as she could.

"Why did you not have sex with her?" Michelle said over the phone as Dana unlocked her apartment door.

"I do not know. Everything seemed creepy. You wouldn't have liked her, anyway."

"Don't base your sexual life on who I may or may not like."

Dana dropped her keys into the bowl on the

counter before petting Mr. Jinx, who always greeted her with a head butt. "I'm not. She reminded me a little too much of Bridge. All I need is another woman who is sexually arrogant to crush my heart. I need to have some sense of dignity, right?"

Michelle added, "You could have at least slept with her and then ghosted her the next day."

Dana poured herself a glass of wine while holding her phone between her cheek and shoulder. "I'm not the ghosting type, but you're right, I should have just slept with her and ended the relationship the next day."

"Now you're talking. You just have to jump into bed with the next woman to get your fancy tickled."

Dana ridiculed the notion. "I don't think so. And good night."

After they said their good nights to one another, Dana took her glass of wine into her bedroom, where she tucked herself into bed for a short buzz-buzz session before drifting off to sleep.

# LODA

*Are you interested in a woman who is strong and sure of herself? I'm 57. A great lover. A hopeless romantic. If you'll let me, I'd love to show you how much I care. Go ahead. Take a chance and send me a message.*

A weekend away was exactly what Dana needed, but it wasn't the relaxing break she craved. In the wee hours of the morning on Saturday, Dana found herself behind the wheel, traveling west on the interstate toward Tampa. Her brother and sister, who both lived there, had called her up and asked her to sign some paperwork regarding a treatment plan for their mother. Even though they could have emailed her the documents, Dana wanted to go visit the nursing home in person. She was the oldest and the one who made most of the decisions regarding their mother's health.

They'd spent their childhood in Tampa. While attending the university in Orlando, Dana developed a deep affection for the city. She never moved back, but she didn't mind driving there for anything they needed. When her father became ill, Dana made the trip multiple times throughout the week. After he passed away, she tried to persuade her mother to sell the house and move to Orlando, where she could keep an eye on her, but their mother refused to leave.

Danielle and Daniel, Dana's identical twin siblings, remained in Tampa as well. Danielle got married soon after she graduated from high school, but they did not have any children together. Daniel was not the type to get married. Always looking for someone better, he jumped from one woman to the next. After the passing of their father, Dana took charge of the family's finances and decisions out of concern Daniel would take advantage of their mother and squander away what little she had.

She didn't necessarily get along very well with her siblings, so on Saturday evening, she sat out on the patio by herself and scouted out the potential dates for her next horrible adventure. At some point, she found herself looking at the profiles and imagining her own scenarios for how the disastrous date would play out. She entertained the idea of writing them down to determine how far off they would be in the event that she ended up going out with them.

She gave the screen a quick glance and saw a woman who appeared to be more of a challenge than anything else. "Loda. A unique name for a naughty woman. What are you going to do on our date? Fart? We'd go play mini golf, and you'd fart the entire time. You'd try to hide it by tapping your club on the ground to make noise, but the smell would tip you off."

"Who the hell are you talking to?"

Dana's train of thought drifted away when she heard a woman's voice coming from behind her. She swiped right on the screen to store Loda's information, before she cast a quick glance behind her to see an elderly woman shuffling toward her with a hunch in her back. "No one, Mama. Just looking at some photos online."

"Why didn't you bring Bridgette with you this weekend?"

The elderly lady sat next to Dana and stroked her leg. Dana said, "Mama, Bridgette and I got a divorce a couple of years ago. We're not together anymore."

"Why would you do such a thing? She reminded me of your father, Charlie."

"Charlie is Dad's brother. You were married to Derek Waites." Her mother's memory loss struck Dana with a tinge of regret.

"You all treat me as though I've lost my mind. I know who your father is; that does not mean I married the son of a bitch."

The concept perplexed Dana, who cocked her head and shot her mother a sidelong glance. "Mama, are you saying Uncle Charlie is my father?"

"Oh, who knows anymore? However, I am curious why you did not bring Bridgette this weekend."

Dana expelled a drawn-out breath. It was rough to see her mother in that state. Perhaps it was advantageous for Dana to be in Orlando. She wished to remember her mother as a sassy woman who always put men in their place.

Loda messaged Dana first thing on Sunday morning. When the message came, she had not yet gotten out of bed. She answered while tucked away in her childhood bedroom, lying under the covers with the door closed. Her bedroom held a great deal of memories. Dana lost her virginity to Summer, who lived on the same street as them. Then, in a brief moment of delirium, she questioned her sexual orientation as a lesbian. She lost her second virginity to a guy named Chester. Very brief because Chester was the one and only man who had ever touched any part of her body. The experiment did nothing but confirm her already established sexuality, which she discovered at a very young age. The only other person who had ever slept in that childhood bed was Bridgette, and even then, it was only occasionally when they were only in town for the night.

If Loda had been present, Dana surely would have enticed her under the sheets. Loda was arrogant. Feminine, but cocky. Perhaps Dana did have a "type," which was a woman so self-assured she compensated for Dana's own lack of self-confidence. During her messages that morning, there was a lot of teasing and flirting going on. The purpose of choosing Loda was not to find true love; rather, it was to get laid. If online dating apps were nothing but a cesspool of one-night stands, she needed to get with the times and start acting like the people she found so annoying. Like Loda, who sent Dana a nude photo of herself. While

Dana ogled at the sexy woman with tattoos defining well-toned torso, Dana declined to stoop to that level and send her one in return. Besides, Dana didn't want to scare Loda off with the pudge around her waist.

On Sunday evening, Dana started the drive back to Orlando. Despite the boastful tone of the profile summary, she consented to meet Loda later that evening. Dana threw those pesky morals out the window after missing out on the opportunity to have potentially amazing sex with a very tall and hot woman. She found a woman who appeared to be someone ready for some mingling.

They planned to meet at a coffee shop in near Loda's home. The strategy called for getting together and determining whether the sparks flew. If they did, Dana would follow Loda back to her house. Dana's anxiety increased throughout the entire ride home. This was not typical behavior for her.

Or maybe it was. She jumped into bed with Summer. Hell, even with Chester. Dana had no remorse for any of the choices she made in the past. Even while she was in college, Dana had a few one-night stands, but Bridgette put an end to all of that. It's possible that the idea of having quick, raunchy sex turned her off because her ex-wife engaged in more frequently than anyone else she knew. Loda might be the sole exception.

Dana deliberated over her decision while she waited for Loda to arrive, and in the end, she took out her phone to cancel the planned meeting. She didn't know Loda well enough, and the idea of just jumping into bed with someone made her feel easy and cheap. The members of the staff refocused their attention on the entrance to the cafe. Along with everyone inside the store, Dana cocked her head to the side in order to see the spectacle just outside the front door.

Police officers dragged an individual away from the building. When Dana realized the person was Loda, her eyes widened. She leaped from her seat and dashed toward the exit in a hurry. Dana pushed the door open slowly as they made eye contact with one another. Loda grinned passively with a smug shrug of her shoulders.

The male officer's eyes darted to her. "Ma'am, go back inside."

Another officer pinned Loda's arms behind her back. When that officer looked up, they made eye contact. Morales.

With no regard for her own safety, Dana stepped forward. "What is happening here? Loda?"

Officer Morales was unequivocal and direct. "Please, go back inside."

"I'm curious why my date is being handcuffed," Dana asserted with a puffed and confident chest.

The male officer yanked Loda backward and placed handcuffs on her wrists. Morales approached Dana in a concerned manner. "Date? The suspect is being charged with domestic assault against her fiancée."

Dana exclaimed to Loda, "Fiancée! You're engaged?"

Loda shook her head as the officer pushed her to

the ground. "I was keeping my options open in case she didn't work out," she yelled back.

Dana made a straight line with her lips and pulled back on her humility. It hurt her dignity for it to take place in front of the hot officer she had a crush on. Dana didn't continue the conversation. Instead, she turned around and pushed her way back inside the coffee shop.

Morales followed her. "Hey. Are you okay?"

She fought back tears, and when she had them under control, Dana turned to Morales. "I'm all right. I suppose that's just a risk of blind dates."

Dana resisted Morales's attempts to console her by pulling away as soon as she felt her gentle hand on her arm. She wanted no emotional support for the level of stupidity she possessed. They both remained silent for longer than Dana wished. Morales finally turned around and continued her pursuit of the wife beater, or to say fiancée beater. While grateful to be on the outside looking in, Dana couldn't shake the feeling the world was conspiring against her happiness.

Dana lifted her head to cast one more glance out the window as she watched Morales pushing Loda into the police car. When Morales shut the door, she faced the front door to the coffee shop. Dana's eyes lowered as soon as Morales took one last sympathetic look at her. Being judged was something she could not stomach. When she finally raised her head, Morales was no longer there. Dana dropped onto the bench next to her and leaned her neck back, resting her head on the cushion. She'd had all she could take.

# CHERYL

*49 SFW. I work in the financial industry.
And even though I enjoy working hard, I always
make time for enjoyment. I like wine, movies,
hiking, and getting out of town on the weekends.
Let's talk to see if we might be a good fit.*

Dana made the long-overdue decision to update her profile to reflect more of her personal taste. It took her over twenty attempts at taking a selfie before she captured an image of herself that did not make her appear overweight and hid her double chin. She wasn't particularly good at taking self-portraits, but she got one that was passable, and she uploaded it along with her updated profile.

Although she did not receive as many responses as she had in the past, the ones that appeared seemed to be more sincere in their hunt for their next true love.

It took Dana longer to choose her next date because she had become extremely exhausted from wasting her time on dates that went nowhere. When

Dana found a woman named Cheryl who seemed to be a good match, she took her time messaging her before agreeing to go out on a date with her.

Their online courtship flourished, winning Dana's heart after almost two weeks of banter back and forth. She divulged more private information about herself than she had previously done with others, such as the name of the flower shop she owned.

On a Friday, just as Dana's florist was about to close up shop for the day, the front door opened. She had to finish a dozen for a customer at the last minute, but she still sprinted around the corner with her knife in hand to greet the customer as soon as they walked in the door. It came as a shock to see Cheryl standing in her doorway.

Dana grinned with a start as her heart rate increased a few notches at the site of Cheryl. "Hi. Um. This is a big surprise. I hadn't expected you."

Cheryl blushed and tilted her head slightly as the spark between them ignited. Her voice paused. "I guess I was curious to see if you were genuine. I figured I'd stop by before asking you out because there are a lot of crazy people online."

"No kidding." Dana motioned her back to her design table. "I'm real. Sorry. I'm making a dozen roses for a gentleman who will return in a few minutes. Do you mind if I work?"

"No. I don't want to interrupt you at all."

"No worries." Dana snipped the stem and placed the purple rose in the vase. "Last minute order. He forgot his anniversary."

Cheryl laughed, her brow furrowed. "Typical guy. I've never seen a rose of that color before. What do you call it?"

"Blueberry. It's the closest thing to purple you'll find. I love it. It has a lovely opening and lasts a long time."

"Very nice. You know, I've never been inside a florist before. This is quite a store you have here." Cheryl took a quick look around the room, as if she were in a foreign land.

The male customer returned to the flower shop; he hovered around her table while Dana arranged a few stems of white limonium into the bouquet. She placed the vase in a box and expressed her gratitude while walking him out to his car with the bouquet. She returned to the design studio and found Cheryl leaning against the table. The sudden flutter in Dana's chest caused her to pause right as she entered the room. Dana noted Cheryl's sandy blonde hair reaching just above her shoulders. She couldn't help but feel a twinge of romantic sap, biting the inside of her bottom lip to calm her breathing.

Cheryl pushed herself away from the table and ambled over to Dana while shrugging her shoulders. "Would you like to go out now that I know you're who you say you are? I was considering going hiking this weekend. More like a nature walk. Want to join me? We can talk, get out of the stuffy indoors?"

Without a pause, Dana blurted out, "Sure. I'd love to go."

"Perfect. Have you ever been to Hal Scott

Preserve?"

"No. I haven't."

"It's stunning. There are a bunch of trails to choose from. What about next Sunday? We can meet there, or I can pick you up. Whichever you prefer."

If she hadn't been on so many disastrous dates, she might have let Cheryl pick her up. "I suppose I could meet you there. If you hate me by the end of the trail, we can part ways."

"I don't think I'll hate you," Cheryl said with a seductive grin on her face. "However, I understand your reluctance. I'll text you the address and meeting location. I'm confident we'll have a good time."

Dana nodded her assent and let Cheryl leave while she tidied up and locked up the store. After getting into her car, she immediately called Michelle and spilled the beans on Cheryl.

Sunday couldn't come soon enough, even though she had a few more conversations with Cheryl before then. Dana put on her sneakers and headed to Hal Scott Preserve, where Cheryl waited for her. Dana's ecstatic grin was impossible to conceal as they exchanged pleasantries.

They started at the trailhead and hiked down a service road to the start of the well-kept path. Many of the swampy areas dried up from the lack of rain in Orlando. Cheryl provided Dana with some background information regarding the nature preserve and the other hiking trails she had explored. Dana admired Cheryl for her love of exploring new places and spending a lot of time outside. It revealed a lot about her relationship with the nature. Even though Dana did little exploring on her own, she could see herself getting into it, particularly if she hiked with an experienced person like Cheryl.

After roughly a mile of walking, Dana noticed she was out of breath and overheated due to the lack of shade on the trail. The sun's rays blazed down on her, even though it was still very early in the morning. The flushing in her cheeks was a visible sign of how out of shape she thought and appeared to be. Dana huffed and puffed her way further along the trail, using conversation to numb the sharp pain shooting through her legs and lungs so as not to interfere with Cheryl's enjoyment.

At about the halfway mark, a bench materialized on the path, and Cheryl invited Dana to sit and give her a chance to regain her breath. Cheryl asked as they sat down together, "Am I walking too fast for you?"

Dana gulped a mouthful of water. "No. I'm just out of shape and need to get out more. I swear I won't be a bad hiking partner after a few more times of this."

"You are not a bad partner at all. Trust me. And I'm enjoying myself with you. It's nice to meet someone who looks like she has her life together."

Dana spat out the water she just consumed. "I wish I had my life together. I've been divorced for four years, and ever since then, it seems like all I attract are a bunch of strange characters—" She retracted her statement. "Not that this or you are strange in any way. In fact, this is the best date I've been on, and I'm having a great time."

Cheryl pushed a strand of Dana's hair out of her eyes. "You look miserable."

Despite the pain radiating from her entire body, Dana's eyes conveyed sincerity. "Not at all. This is nice."

Dana arose from the bench with a groan as soon as she seemed ready to continue. Her legs burned with each step. Cheryl laughed. "Do you need to be carried back?"

Dana said to herself, "Walk it off, Waites."

"Dana Waites? I like the last name."

Cheryl suddenly leaned in close to Dana and gave her a gentle peck on the lips unexpectedly. And in that instant, Dana forgot about the pain ripping through the nerves of her legs. A tickle in her stomach cured all of her ailments. Dana joked, "Maybe I do want you to carry me out after that."

"Let's go slow, and I'll give you another one when we get back to the trailhead."

They continued on their way back to the starting point, but didn't bring up the kiss again. Dana's excitement level reached an all-time high when they finally reached the end of their loop and could see their cars. "I made it!"

"You did!" Cheryl checked her watch and said, "A tad over four miles. For a minute there, I thought I needed to call a medic."

Dana swatted her arm and leaned against her car. "Whatever. I made it. That's all that's important."

"And just as promised." Cheryl stepped close and

pressed her lips against Dana's, taking her time to savor the moment.

"A woman of her word," Dana said as Cheryl drew away slightly. "That was nice."

"Does that mean there might be a second date?"

Dana didn't want the kiss to end. She finally found someone worthy of her time. "I'm sure a second date is inevitable. Without a doubt."

"Glad to hear it. Are your legs gonna get you home?"

"I think I'll be fine, though I'm not sure they'll let me out of the car when I arrive."

"Okay. So, if you need help standing, call me and I'll come running." Cheryl said goodbye with another quick kiss. "We'll talk and set up another date that doesn't involve a wheelchair."

"Deal." Dana waved as Cheryl walked to her car. She slid into hers and turned on the engine. They both drove away in opposite directions.

After a few days of exchanging messages, Dana invited Cheryl to visit her at her home, where she could prepare dinner for the two of them and converse in an atmosphere free from the distractions by other people. On that day, Dana left work early and scrubbed her apartment from top to bottom while her anxiety levels skyrocketed through the roof.

Dana found herself to be out of her element as the clock ticked down to Cheryl's arrival, not usually being forward enough to initiate such an intimate meeting. Because of her obsessive-compulsive disorder, she over cleaned everything to where there was literally no more time.

She ran as fast as she could to take a shower. As she washed all of her lady parts, Michelle's comments about jumping into bed with the next person kept playing in her head as she prepared for the possibility that it would. Still rushing to get ready, she primped as she could until there was a knock on the door.

When Cheryl came in and kissed Dana hello, Dana inhaled the sweet scent of warm vanilla sugar that Cheryl brought into the house. Dana caught her breath and exhaled as she almost melted from their closeness.

After a quick tour of the place, they adjourned to the kitchen, where Dana had dinner simmering on the stove.

"Oh my goodness, it smells divine in here. I haven't had a home-cooked meal in a long time. I'm not a good cook, so I usually grab something on the way home," Cheryl said as she glanced over Dana's shoulder while Dana stirred.

The last time someone stood over her shoulder in the kitchen, Bridgette griped about how she'd made minestrone soup for the millionth time. Hearing the gratitude in Cheryl's voice made her feel grateful to have someone appreciate her efforts.

"You mentioned you liked wine. There is red on the counter and white in the refrigerator. Pour some for yourself. The glasses are in the cabinet beside it."

Cheryl complied with Dana's request and took out two glasses from the cabinet, as though she was familiar with their exact location. Cheryl did not show the least bit of reluctance as she opened a drawer, located the corkscrew, then opened the bottle of red wine.

"You appear to be a red woman." Cheryl handed Dana the freshly poured glass, then poured another for herself.

"Yes. I am. I much prefer a good Pinot Noir." Dana took a sip, then set the glass next to her while Cheryl leaned against the counter behind her, watching her cook.

Mr. Jinx leaped onto the countertop. "Go on," Dana said as she pushed him away. "No cats allowed on the counter when guests are present. You know that."

"Kittens are uncontrollable. They do as they please."

"There's no doubt about it." Mr. Jinx jumped across the room, landed next to Cheryl on the counter, and nudged her arm with a head butt. Dana took notice. "He's taken with you."

"Excellent judge of character, if I might say," Cheryl teased with a seductive grin.

Dana ignored her trembling hands and reached for her confidence as she said, "His mom likes you too."

"I'm delighted to hear that." Cheryl pushed Dana away from the counter and reached around her waist, snuggling in. "I can't wait to try this."

The innuendo fueled the already simmering sexual tension in the kitchen. Dana took a few deep breaths and let her eyes slowly close as she savored the sensation of another woman's body pressing up against hers. Her vocal cords let out a pathetic little whimper. When it did, the embarrassment caused a flush to her face.

Cheryl untied her arms from around Dana's waist. "Do I make you nervous?"

"A little, but that's not necessarily a bad thing." Dana took the bowls and plates from the cupboard and began plating the food. "Have a seat, and I'll bring you dinner."

Cheryl brought their wine glasses to the table for them. After Cheryl had taken a seat, Dana placed the plate with the smothered chicken and wild rice in front of her. Besides that, she set a bowl of Caesar salad in the center of the table. She took her seat across from Cheryl, where she had her own place setting. The two women ate in silence, trying to ignore the sultry chemistry between them.

Following the meal, Dana discarded the soiled plates into the sink, intending to clean them after Cheryl left that night. They carried their wine glasses with them into the living room, where they sat down together on the couch. It took almost an hour before the uncomfortable silence set in. Instead of speaking, Dana could only laugh. The anxiety to keep the words flowing caused a tightness in her chest, almost close to hyperventilating.

"What's so funny?" Cheryl asked.

She shook her head and tossed her pestering moral convictions out the window. "We both know where this is going, so instead of looking for topics to muddle through, we should just let it happen."

"True. I'd like that, but it's perfectly fine if you're not ready. No pressure," Cheryl said.

It was Cheryl's casual approach that eased them into them ripping their clothes off as they made their way to the bedroom. Both of them without shirts, Dana pushed Cheryl backward on the bed. She pulled off the pair of jeans that were standing in the way of what Dana needed. Cheryl's underwear came off with the jeans; she reached for Dana and pulled her onto the bed. After Cheryl disrobed Dana, she climbed atop her and wiggled her way between Dana's legs.

As she opened up to Cheryl, Dana squeezed her lips together. She didn't want to come across as a moaner, especially on their first date. The whimpers of pleasure escaped when she came so abruptly. She nearly forgot how wonderful it felt, as it had been so long since anyone had been down there. When she came, her eyes closed tightly to hide the embarrassment of not lasting more than a few minutes.

Cheryl finished kissing Dana all the way up her body and finally reached her lips. Dana's heavy breathing stopped, but the flushing of her cheeks had not. "I'm sorry that was so quick," Dana apologized.

"No worries, babe. It's better than you not coming and bruising my ego."

*How could Cheryl be so perfect?* Dana lifted a hand to Cheryl's face and pulled her close, pressing their lips together. Dana turned their bodies around with such ease. She moved her mouth over Cheryl's body, gliding downward until she reached Cheryl's core. She savored the flavor of a woman as Cheryl's sex sent her mouth agape, and she gloried in the experience. Something she desperately needed.

Dana enjoyed every aspect of that part of sex as she flicked her tongue, but then she heard something so unexpected. As Cheryl made the most peculiar sound, Dana's eyes widened, and her ministerial motions slowed down. Dana tried to redirect her focus back to the pleasurable act as the strange groan grew louder.

A gurgling noise, like Cheryl gargled mouthwash, came from above her. The sound increased proportionately as Dana continued to please the woman below her. Dana understood people had various ways of expressing joy; some were extremely boisterous and vocal, and offered commentary along the way. While she, along with others, repressed her pleasures, others did the opposite; perhaps Cheryl's way was an innovative approach.

While Dana worked her way toward providing Cheryl with a memorable orgasm, Cheryl rotated her pelvis and buckled her hips. Cheryl's vibrating purr reverberated off the bedroom walls as she reached her climax. Cheryl let out a load of pulsating cries as she reached her peak. The sound was eerily reminiscent of a giant wookiee howling out in agony.

Dana did her best to contain her laughter as she listened to her partner emit a thrumming growl. When it became too much, Dana stopped so Cheryl would silence her excitement. She crept up from between Cheryl's legs and wiped her mouth with the back of her hand, but when she dropped back onto the bed, she found it difficult to look the woman in the eyes.

"Whoa," Cheryl said, as Dana tried to process whatever came out of Cheryl's mouth. "I haven't orgasmed so hard in such a long time. You certainly know what you're doing."

Dana did not know what she had done to cause a woman to make such a hideous noise. One that nearly scared her because Dana thought the woman next to her convulsed and choked on her own spit. No words came out of her mouth. She couldn't think of any words that weren't rude or derogatory.

As soon as Cheryl rolled onto her back, she moved her hands to Dana's stomach and readied for the next round. Dana flinched in disgust as a swarm of creepy crawlers scurried over her and itched her skin. She said, "One is my max a night. I'm spent."

"Good to know. Next time, I'll have to make it count. Slow down to get the full experience." With a swift movement, Cheryl tore her hand from Dana's body and pushed herself up from the mattress. "God. Wow. I think we both desperately needed that."

Dana, still speechless, pondered what the hell came out of Cheryl's mouth during sex and dreaded the concept of a next time. "Yeah, probably."

"Normally, I'm not one to rush into bed, but when the time is right, the time is right," Cheryl explained as she dressed.

Seeing Cheryl in front of her changing, a flood of regret washed over Dana. How quickly a roll in the sheets happened and how dirty she felt. Everything had gone so well until sex. Until Cheryl opened her mouth with crying out in a horrendous extraterrestrial howl. And at that moment, Dana leaped from the bed and hurried to dress as remorse reddened her cheeks.

Cheryl sensed Dana's discomfort. "I hope you don't come to regret sleeping together so soon. If we're going too fast, we can slow down."

"We probably should." Dana said as twisted away from Cheryl's gaze. When Cheryl extended her hand to her, Dana pulled it away in disgust. She lied. "I'm sorry. Just so many memories of my ex are coming back to me and I feeling very—"

Cheryl backed away, helping her out of a confession of emotions. "It's cool. Am I the first since your divorce?"

"Yes." That wasn't a lie.

Cheryl nodded said good night to Dana with respect so she could reflect. "I understand the first time after a breakup," Cheryl said at the door, "so take your time and call me when you want to go out again."

Dana, without looking her in the eye, thanked her and closed the door. Once alone, she shook the creepiness from her body and exclaimed, "What the hell was that?"

# MICHELLE

D ana and Michelle sat next to each other on the patio of a small bistro in downtown Orlando. "I'm serious. When she came, the woman sounded like Chewbacca." Dana's statement did not convince Michelle, so she repeated it.

Michelle laughed as she tried to make excuses for the woman. "Perhaps she had a cold and phlegm globber got stuck in her throat."

"No. Her body manifested the spirit of a wookiee, which is a deal breaker."

Michelle took another look at Cheryl's profile on Dana's phone. "Don't say that. You really liked this one. I'm sure you're exaggerating."

"Really? I thought for sure she would cough up a hairball at any second."

"So, you're really not going to go out with her again?"

"I can't. Even though she checked off a lot of the boxes on my list of ideal partners, there are some things I just can't get past. One of them is gargling during sex."

Michelle shook her head as she returned the phone to Dana, disagreeing with Dana's reasoning. "How are you going to end things with her?"

"I kind of hoped you'd help me with that." Dana tucked her shoulders into herself, her eyes begging.

"No. Nope. Maybe if I agreed with you, but I believe you are being too critical. You've finally met someone you like; a serious contender to replace Bridgette, and you're just looking for an excuse not to get involved with them."

Over the course of their relationship, Dana had often wished Michelle played for the opposing team. If Michelle were a lesbian, that solved all her problems, but alas, she wasn't. The benefits of having a partner outweighed those a best friend provided. That essential missing ingredient was human sexual contact. Dana's favorite vibrator satisfied her need for stimulation, but what she really craved was some quality one-on-one time.

"This is not some ruse to remain single. I want to be in a relationship. Michelle, I'm serious about Cheryl. If you don't trust me, go hook up with her," Dana continued, pleading her case.

"Fine. Break up with her, but don't ask me for help."

Dana rolled her eyes. "Whatever! I will not remind you of all the times I helped you in getting rid of your revolving door of guys when we first met?"

Huffing, Michelle took Dana's phone and began typing a message with a few clicks. She read it as she typed, "Hey. As much as I enjoyed our time together, I believe I need to devote some time to self-care. Spending time with you triggered some internal emotions. I need to work through them before considering a relationship. I'm sorry, but it's something I have to do."

As Michelle pressed the send button, a twisting sensation developed in Dana's stomach. It felt terrible to end things with someone she liked before they had even become a couple.

Michelle slid the phone back. "It's not a lie. You're still hung up on Bridgette. You're not opening yourself up to love again. Not every girl will break your heart."

In every way, Dana and Michelle should never have been friends. If the boxes on the scorecard were to be checked off for commonalities, the card would be completely empty. They shared nothing in common, but at the same time, neither one of them functioned properly without the other. And they'd never even fought; that was the cherry on top.

When Dana moved to Orlando while attending college, that was when they first met. She moved into the same apartment complex in which Michelle lived. They were next-door neighbors who shared an apartment directly opposite one another. Although they did not become friends right away, it took about three rowdy all-night parties, which Dana found annoying and loud, before they became friends.

On the morning following Dana's third complaint regarding the noise, Michelle arrived at Dana's door with a peace offering in the form of a coffee cake and knocked on her door. Although there were no conditions associated with the cake, Dana found herself at Michelle's apartment later that day, cleaning up her damaged living room. After that point, they became inseparable and have remained so ever since. Therefore, it came as no surprise Michelle was always privy to the nitty-gritty details of Dana's life.

They had been each other's rocks each time their dating lives took a turn for the worse, and they celebrated the moments of joy when things went right, such as Dana's wedding. When Scott started hanging out with them at the local watering hole, he quickly became one of their closest friends. Though he shared in the more recent memories, Michelle was Dana's person.

If Dana fell in love with someone else, that person must first gain Michelle's approval before becoming Dana's significant other. After Bridgette, Michelle demanded it. To begin with, she hadn't exactly been on board with the couple's romantic involvement. Michelle had a good sense of judgment regarding people's personalities, and she voiced her disapproval frequently whenever Dana and Bridgette butted heads.

Dana planned to go home after her brunch with Michelle, but she didn't make it. She drove to Hal Scott Preserve while feeling extremely depressed. At the trailhead, she attempted to think back on her date with Cheryl as she sat in her car. Perhaps she had imagined the unpleasant sexual experience. Was there an unconscious, underlying fear about getting involved with someone else again?

Dana frequently sought Michelle's counsel, which,

nine times out of ten, turned out to be correct. What are the odds of her being correct about Cheryl? After retrieving her phone, Dana navigated her way back to Cheryl's profile. Dana's inability to commit to this perfect woman after their first date defied logic.

The message Michelle sent to Cheryl was only a band-aid until Dana decided whether she wanted to end the relationship for good. Dana's life over the past few months had become increasingly reminiscent of Michelle's life in her earlier years. Revolving men. Or in Dana's case, revolving women. Since she started going out on dates again, she met a movie snob, sex goddess, a wife beater, and the rest of the ensemble of crazy characters.

Dana dug deep within herself to discover where she might have misunderstood them and how she could fix it, so she wasn't the problem. After considering each of them, she thought about Cheryl again. She eventually needed to decide because Cheryl would reply to the message and want to check in.

The awkwardness of having to decide whether you like someone was the aspect of dating she disliked the most. She agonized over every choice as if it were the end of the world if she didn't decide quickly after the first date with each potential partner. Dana didn't need to decide. The world would not end if she took a moment to let people simmer on her stove. Before making a choice, Cheryl needed to marinate a little longer. In the meantime, it was imperative that she stop stressing about women.

Dana got out of the car and walked to the trailhead

and beyond. She didn't have hiking gear on, but she had a pair of running shoes on. That was fine because she walked onto the dirt path to meditate and take in the scenery.

# MYA

*My name is Mya, and if I had to describe myself in three words, they would be cheerful, a little reserved, and a big laugher. Okay, there were a few extra words, but it's fun to break the rules sometimes.*

**C**heerful. Reserved. Laugher. These were all characteristics Dana found attractive in a woman. Mya was a bit too butch for her, but after Michelle called her out for not being open to love, Dana decided to be less judgmental about appearances.

They got together at an Irish restaurant in Disney Springs, which was not an area Dana particularly desired to go to on the weekend. Every Disney location faced its own unique set of difficulties on account of the considerable number of visitors every day. Dana stayed away from Disney like the plague for several reasons, including the lengthy walks, the crowded sidewalks, and the overpriced food. The only reason she agreed to meet Mya was because Michelle's persistent voice kept telling her she was closed off and extremely picky about the women she dated.

As she walked into the restaurant, a bead of sweat ran down the side of her cheek. The sudden rush of cold air left her with a pleasant tingling sensation that was just what she needed to combat the oppressive heat of the day.

As she approached, Mya hopped up from the waiting area. "Dana. Hi. I'm Mya."

Dana extended her hand out, and a giggle hidden behind her lips at Mya's touristy outfit of a Disney shirt and mouse ears. "Hello. It's a pleasure to meet you."

The hostess led them to their table, a quiet booth in the restaurant's back corner. "Thank you for meeting me," Mya said as she slid in opposite Dana. "This is the only place at Disney Springs I haven't eaten at, so thank you for bringing me."

There had been no prior discussion regarding the practical aspects of the date. Dana didn't bring her, but she did ask Mya out, so there was an automatic assumption Dana would pay. Fine. She dismissed the remark with a casual shrug as the waiter brought the table some waters. Dana guzzled the majority before he even stepped away from the table because the walk had left her sweaty and parched.

Dana knew Mya was a Disney fan based on their conversation over messaging apps. Because of her attire, she most likely was a fanatic. "You've eaten at every restaurant over here?" Dana asked.

"Except this one, but that will change today."

"I know you said you enjoyed visiting Disney

World, but you seem completely immersed in the Disney experience."

Mya's eyes twinkled with delight. "It's the entire reason I moved to Orlando. It was either here or to California, which is far too expensive. Orlando is still too expensive for me, but there is so much more to do here."

"I believe both states have their advantages. After college, I spent a year in San Diego. I might have stayed on the west coast if it hadn't been for my family," Dana added, shifting the conversation away from the mouse.

Mya reintroduced the subject. "San Diego would have been too far away from Disneyland. I'd have to move to Anaheim, but it's far too expensive. I keep applying for jobs with them, but I never get a call back."

She'd just go with it. "What position did you apply for?" Dana asked.

"Many. I really want to be a photopass photographer, but I'll take a ride or do something anything else. I just really want to work for them."

"I'm not sure what a photopass is, but a photographer? Do you enjoy taking photographs?" Dana asked, looking for something else they might have in common. Dana considered herself a photography hobbyist, with a few old school cameras and shoe boxes full of photographs she had taken over the years.

"No. Not at all." Mya's words flew out of her mouth so quickly they didn't register as a blip on her radar of interest. Dana found it strange that a woman who had no interest in photography wanted to be a photographer.

The waiter arrived at the table and took their order. When he left, Dana continued to play twenty questions, hoping the conversation would go in a different direction. However, every time Mya answered, she added something Disney to it, almost as if she had an unhealthy fixation on the company.

Over the course of her life, Dana had also encountered many devoted Disney fans. In Orlando, it wasn't all that unusual for people to relocate closer to the city's many amusement parks, particularly after they retired. Mya was a lot younger than Dana, so she wasn't close to retirement age; however, Dana had a hard time figuring out what Mya did for a living. It had to be a direct question. "What do you do for a living, Mya?"

"Right now, nothing. Like I said, I've been looking for work here, but can't seem to get an interview," Mya responded.

The rest of the lunch was more of the same. Lots of conversations. There was nothing tangible linking them, so when the check arrived, Dana pulled out her wallet and threw the credit card on the receipt.

Mya made no offer to pay even a fraction of the bill. "Thanks for lunch," she said instead. "It was delicious."

"You're very welcome." Dana couldn't say much more without sounding rude.

"I would like to repay you for lunch. If you want to

come back to my house, we can watch a movie and I'll thank you for lunch."

Once more, Michelle's words about being shut off echoed in Dana's head like a broken record. She gave Michelle's list of possible responses to the situation some thought. After that, she gave Scott's viewpoint some serious consideration. Both of her best friends would have ended up at this person's house and hooking up, especially since that was what Mya ultimately wanted from her. Food, a movie and a thank you.

She was not that kind of person. Her moral compass pointed her in a different direction than her friends, but Dana didn't have a person, while her closest friends had numerous people in their lives. Dana looked around the restaurant as she decided, thinking that might be her biggest issue. At long last, she stared Mya dead in the eyes before hurling all of her core beliefs out the open window. "Sure. Why not?"

They quietly left the booth and elbowed their way through the waiting diners to the front door. Dana danced between people to get to the sidewalk, but the sudden blast of summer heat nearly choked her. Her gaze darted around in search of Mya, who appeared behind her and attempted to wrap her arms around Dana.

Dana jumped, her face turning bright white from being startled and afraid of crowds. Mya's pupils constricted with concern. "I'm sorry; I didn't mean to scare you."

Dana gripped her chest, slowing her heartbeat. "No. It's just me. I'm fine."

They walked toward the parking lot, with Mya trailing behind sluggishly. When Mya did not cross the parking lot toward the parked cars, Dana arched her brow in surprise.

"Where are you parked?" Dana asked from the other side of the road. Dana's phone alerted her to a text message, and she saw Mya's number pop up.

Mya yelled out. "I just texted you my address. Do you want to meet there in an hour or so? I'm awaiting an Uber."

The oddness of the day increased by the minute. "Do you need a ride?" Dana asked. "I mean, I assumed that was the plan to head to your place. I can drive you home if you don't have a car."

"I don't want to impose. You already bought lunch."

Dana returned across the drive to meet Mya. "I can drive you home if you need a ride," Dana said, being a nice person. "There's no need to call a ride."

Mya asked, "You sure?"

"Of course."

Mya followed Dana to her car. She entered the coordinates into the GPS and allowed the dash to provide her with directions while Mya continued to express her gratitude for the ride. Finally, they arrived at the house where Dana parked in front. It was by no means a modest house. In a desirable neighborhood, the ranch-style residence had a well-kept yard. It boded well to learn Mya led a comfortable life;

particularly given she didn't really have a job at the moment.

Dana asked, "You live alone?"

"Nah. I'm just staying here until I get accepted by Disney, at which point I'll be able to live on the property with the other cast members."

"Are you staying with relatives? Friends?" Again, the date turned into a bizarre and twisted tale. Dana didn't want to judge and tell Michelle she had failed again.

"It's a friend's house, but don't worry. No one is at home." Mya pushed open the car door and motioned Dana out. "We'll have the place to ourselves."

Dana gave a low nod as she followed, getting out of the car, and walking in the house's direction. Mya climbed the stairs with an air of brazen self-assurance and unlocked the front door. "Please excuse the mess. We have a lot of people living here, but I try to keep my area as clean as possible."

Dana stepped over a blanket and navigated around children's toys in the living room. She accompanied Mya to the rear of the house. The sudden appearance of a futon in the kitchen caused Dana's eyes to snap open in startled surprise. A big television faced the seating area was on the counter. Mya took the nearby remote control and turned on the console.

Dana hesitated, suddenly realizing she made a mistake by agreeing to meet this person after their date. They were clearly going to sit on the futon in the kitchen to watch their movie. Mya waved her hands in the air as Dana sat down. "Whoa! Wait! Don't sit down yet."

Dana jerked upward instead of sitting down. Mya opened a drawer filled with items not intended for kitchen use. Mya pulled out a lint roller and ran it over Dana's shirt and pants. "You have a cat, don't you?"

"I do," Dana said, watching the woman's hand scroll up and down, cleaning the stray cat hairs on Dana's clothing.

She finished and motioned for Dana to finally sit. "You're good. It's just that I sleep here and don't want any pet hair if possible."

Dana dismissed the thought with a wave of her hand and sat down on the futon. Mya sat down next to her, prompting Dana to move a little to put some distance between them, but she wound up sitting on the plush crab doll from *The Little Mermaid*. Dana shifted her weight to reach the stuffed animal hiding under her, then flung it away.

Following the appearance of the recognizable castle logo at the beginning of the film, the animated scenes from the movie Aladdin played on the screen. As Dana grimaced at the prospect of watching a cartoon, she reached behind her head and rubbed the back of her neck. Dana's eyes traveled around the room as she took in the surroundings, noticing they were in a kitchen, complete with a range and a sink. Even though there was a walkway behind the futon where one could cook and do the dishes, the futon took up most of the space in the room.

Mya's lack of a bedroom perplexed her. "How many people live here?"

Mya answered, "Five." After she finished speaking, she hit the rewind button so they could watch the part of the movie they missed because Dana asked a question. Better than her date with Britt, during which the woman hushed her whenever she opened her mouth to speak.

Dana glanced at her watch in disbelief, hoping time had passed since she last checked it, but the hands remained motionless as the movie played on.

When the main characters of the moved kissed, Mya mentioned to Dana, "This part gets me every time."

After finishing her sentence, Mya leaned close to Dana and planted a passionate kiss on her. Mya took advantage of her dominant position to climb on top of Dana, pushing her backward under the weight of her body. Dana allowed it to happen, but the uncomfortable feeling of a plush crab biting into her back made the entire situation seem surreal.

There was plenty of passion in the kiss. Mya's hands, slick with desire, explored Dana's body and slid beneath her clothing. Within a matter of seconds, Mya cupped Dana's breasts and gave them a firm squeeze while their lips remained locked together. Mya's hand slid downward, grazing Dana's pudgy stomach until it reached the button of Dana's pants. The button opened with a swift flip, and Mya quickly hunted for Dana's center. As soon as Mya dipped between her folds, Dana immediately buckled her hips upward and took everything Mya wanted to give.

Dana squealed as Mya brought her to the brink,

which was a much more enjoyable experience than Cheryl's short romp of gargling. Her mouth gaped open when she hit her peak, letting out a long-winded whimper. Mya didn't take her hand from Dana's sex as she drew back to admire the look of satisfaction in her eyes. Mya said, "Thanks for lunch and *Aladdin* sex."

There was a delay in the delivery of a response. Mostly because the decent sex, which surprised Dana, left her speechless. She hadn't expected it to be good, and she didn't expect it to come that hard. Dana couldn't help but crack a wry smile at the irony of the fact a movie, let alone a cartoon, turned someone on.

Mya wiggled her fingers again. Dana allowed herself another round as she lowered her head and pressed her hips upward into Mya's hand. But as she closed her eyes to enjoy the ride, the sound of the front door creaking open caused Dana's eyes to pop wide open. She contorted her body to get out from under Mya.

"Don't worry. It's most likely one of the guys." Mya continued without pausing the momentum.

Dana snatched Mya's arm from under her pants. "Let's not do this."

To look presentable, she straightened her posture and buttoned her pants. Dana jumped up from the sofa as soon as a tall man with unkempt hair and a beard entered the kitchen. Dana rushed at her words. "I should go. It's been fun. I'll call you."

Dana dashed through the house, hopping over the plethora of children's toys scattered throughout the living room, and out the front door into the sweltering heat of the afternoon. The moment she hit the driveway; a minivan stuffed with young children arrived. Youngsters with high-pitched excitement piled out of the car alongside a stocky woman whose hips gave the impression she birthed all of them.

Dana didn't bother to wait around to be introduced; instead, she dashed off in her car as soon as she got the chance. A dramatic sigh escaped her lips as she expressed relief she hadn't been in the midst of a second orgasm when the kids came running into the house.

The next day at work, Dana focused her attention on the paperwork she needed to complete, but a customer who required floral arrangements interrupted her. The front door opened once more in the middle of their planning session. When Dana glanced up at the door, she discovered it wasn't actually a customer at all. The moment Cheryl walked through the storefront door, a punch in Dana's stomach sucked all the air out of her lungs.

Dana made an excuse to her actual customer and marched over to Cheryl, grabbing her by the arm and dragging her to the side of the room. "What are you doing here?"

"I know you said you needed some time, but I just wanted to check in on you. See how you were doing." Cheryl spoke while giving off a sweet smile and a sympathetic look.

While it was thoughtful of Cheryl to check in on her, she hadn't expected it. Her words became entangled in a lump in her throat. "I'm fine, but with a client. I'll call you?"

Dana distanced herself from Cheryl deliberately. She hoped Cheryl would walk away with each step she took toward her client. Instead, Cheryl browsed the wares while meandering aimlessly throughout the store. Dana exhaled deeply as she walked back to the counter to continue working with the client on the event's logistics.

After they finished, the customer started walking out the door. Dana almost choked on air as another person entered the store. Mya waved, making a direct line to Dana and saying, "So this is where you work. It's a really cool place."

Dana's voice cracked as she struggled to deal with the awkwardness of the last two people she had sex with confronting her at the same time. "Yes. Hi. This is my store."

Dana lowered her voice as she slipped from around the counter to Mya, noting Mya's Disney's Jasmine tee shirt. It only served as a reminder of a line she never should have crossed. "Um. I hope this doesn't come across as rude, but I'm working. Unless you need some flowers."

Mya raised her head. "I came to see if you were okay because you hadn't returned my messages after running out the door."

She pursed her lips tightly, in over her head with two women she didn't want to see again. She hadn't responded to Mya's messages because she was doing exactly what she despised with others. Dana ghosted

Mya. "I'm fine. It's just a terribly busy day. I'll message you later."

Dana twisted out of the way as Mya leaned in to kiss her. Dana's eyes widened in confusion as the situation left both of the women perplexed. "I'm at work," Dana attempted to whisper.

When Dana's gaze shifted toward Cheryl, Mya followed suit. They both stared at Cheryl's presence. Mya understood when she nodded. "Oh. There's someone else?"

Dana clenched her fists as bile rose in her stomach. She opened them, turned Mya to the door, and put a hand on her back to lead her out. "No. Please. I'll call you."

Dana, seeing Mya leave, turned slowly, bracing herself to deal with yet another woman she didn't want in her shop. "I'm just not ready to get into anything serious, Cheryl."

As she turned, Cheryl replaced the ceramic floral picture frame on the shelf. She huffed a stifled laugh. "I'm sure you weren't taking her seriously, either."

Dana opened her mouth to defend herself but quickly shut it and bowed her head in shame. She walked toward Cheryl, feeling exceptionally low and pitiful, knowing she needed to explain. Dana looked up at Cheryl and said, "Clearly, I'm not ready to date because I've made a lot of bad choices recently, and I regret every one of them."

"Clearly." Cheryl took a step around Dana and marched toward the door, slamming it shut.

Feeling defeated, Dana took to the front door,

locked it, and flipped on the closed sign. As she turned into her store, she looked around at her life and wondered how she got into that spot. She leaned against the door, sat down, and tucked her knees into her chest. She needed to quit dating.

# BRIDGETTE

Dana stayed away from the dating scene and, unfortunately, her friends for the following month. She claimed to be busy at work, allowing her ample time for self-care. She believed the consequences of ignoring her internal moral compass bit her in the ass. In the end, the two girls she jumped into bed with confronted her, and all that did was make Dana feel worse about herself. When she finally finished her self-loathing, she opened the dating app and gave it a look, only to swipe left to get rid of almost every profile the app suggested.

Once and for all, she deleted the program from her phone and tossed it aside. She found it oddly comforting to go out, although she had spent the previous few months on many unsatisfactory dates. She at least could claim to be part of the dating scene. Dana grew increasingly lonely as Mr. Jinx kneaded the blanket and purred next to her. As she listened to his quiet hum, a tear welled up in her eye. She wished Bridgette were sitting next to her, grumbling about something trivial.

Dana cast her gaze over to the opposite side of the couch. Bridgette's spot. When she moved out, she took the sofa with her, and it carried a lot of memories with it. After they got divorced, Bridgette gave Dana first dibs on whatever she wanted to keep from their shared belongings. As the couple vacated their city penthouse, Bridgette took possession of all the unwanted items. Dana huffed a sigh of loneliness seeing the empty seat once occupied by her former wife. She went to bed, completely devoid of all feeling, even an ounce of happiness.

The following morning, Dana pulled into the parking lot of the all-too-familiar office building rather than going to the flower shop. A replay of the fight that ultimately led to the end of her marriage played in her head as she gazed upward to the tenth floor. She blinked her eyes several times, willing herself to gather the energy necessary to return to Bridgette's workplace.

Given that it was also once her office, she had a poor chance of avoiding recognizable faces. She let out a gasp before stepping out of the vehicle and making her way to the infamous tenth floor.

The company sign welcomed her as the elevator doors opened, but there was no one at the front desk. It was good to see that some things remained unchanged. To save their lives, the company never retained a receptionist longer than a week. Dana pushed open the double glass doors and hurried toward the offices. Faces and heads turned in her direction as soon as the doors opened, but no one intervened to stop her. They never stop people who walked purposefully into the office. People frequently stopped and questioned those who dallied.

Through the clear glass office walls, Dana noticed no one else in Bridgette's office with her. Bridgette had already noticed her when she knocked on the glass wall. Bridgette's expression of shock as Dana opened the door was priceless. "Hey," Dana said as she shut the door behind her. "Can we talk?"

"Well, this is a surprise I never expected to see you again, especially here," Bridgette said, emerging from behind her desk to greet Dana.

Dana scoffed at the remark, lifting her shoulder. "Well, yeah. I never expected to return, but here I am."

"Talk? That's a loaded gun for sure. Everything okay?"

Despite their disagreements, Bridgette wasn't resentful of their split. This was Dana's job. Perhaps Dana insisted on the divorce for this reason. When Dana first learned about the affair, Bridgette's casual attitude toward the cheating irritated her. Bridgette never begged her to stay or offered to change. Instead of fighting for answers, Dana took it as evidence that Bridgette did not care.

Perhaps it was time to ask the questions they had avoided. "How come you cheated on me?"

Bridgette cocked her head, almost taking a step back. Her pupils constricted with worry. "Where is this coming from, Dane? It's been nearly five years."

Dana's question and her steps backward toward past heartache were like a knife slicing through her chest. "I'm sorry. This is ridiculous. I'm gonna go."

Bridgette reached for Dana's hand as she

approached the door to prevent her from leaving. "Wait. Dane. What's going on?"

Dana hadn't heard the voice that always lit her heart on fire shorten her name in an awfully long time. Dana turned around, leaped forward, and encircled Bridgette with her arms. Their quick embrace resulted in a passionate kiss that weakened Dana's knees. While they kissed, nothing else seemed to matter, but when it was over, their history hit Dana like a freight train. Reality settled in her chest.

"Fuck!" As she pushed away, Dana said, "I'm such an idiot. I need to go."

Seeing Dana hesitant, Bridgette reached out a hand and gently enticed her fingers to join hers. "You've always been the best kisser."

Dana's tone abruptly shifted to sarcasm. "Just not good enough to keep you."

Bridgette snatched Dana's hand as she leaned back against her desk. "I don't think you came all the way up here to scream at me about something that happened years ago. Why are you really here, Dane?"

As soon as she withdrew her hand from Bridgette's, she reached up to automatically adjust Bridgette's collar of her dress shirt. Bridgette kept her hand close but withdrew it. Dana repented after realizing what she had done.

"Would you like me to shut the blinds?" Bridgette cracked a joke.

Dana's laughter disrupted the moment. "Fine. I've begun dating again, and it's a complete joke. They are either complete idiots or so strange that I can't imagine being with them."

"And? You're curious why it isn't working. So that's why you wanted to know why I cheated."

Bridgette was the opposite of everyone on her recent dating calendar. Bridgette always had herself one step ahead of conversations and deals because of her keen sense of awareness. Dana admired this aspect of Bridgette's personality. "Why wasn't I ever good enough for you?"

"Did you ever consider I wasn't good enough for you?" Bridgette's laughter echoed off the walls.

"No, because you were."

"Yeah. I wasn't, babe. I knew the moment I met you. You were all prim and proper, and completely out of my league."

"I wasn't exactly prim and proper." Dana arched her brows downward. "You were simply a corporate hungry kiss-ass who knew exactly where she wanted to be."

"On top. On top of the company. On top of all the women in the office, including you; especially you. Dane, I tried. I really did. It just wasn't in me. It wasn't anything you did, trust me."

Dana took a step back and paced the room. "Michelle thinks I'm comparing everyone to you," Dana said with her back to Bridgette.

"You might be, but I wouldn't do it. I'm a dog, and you know it." Dana swung around to hear Bridgette finish her statement. "You have so much to offer people, Dane. Perhaps you're being too picky because you always want the best—"

Dana cut her off. "No, I don't."

Pushing herself away from the desk, Bridgette let out a guttural laugh. "Look at our lives, Dane. Where do you shop? What do you wear? Hell, because of you, my closet has more zeros than most."

"You act as if all I think about is money and expensive things?" Dana puffed up her chest, offended by Bridgette's assessment of her tastes.

"And grandiose romantic gestures. You're looking for a fairytale that doesn't exist. People. Love. Relationships. It's all a mess, and you're not a messy person. You've never been one to accept things that aren't perfect."

Dana's eyes lowered to the ground as Bridgette read her like a book. Unfortunately, everything she said was true, which was the reason she couldn't believe Bridgette's infidelity. She didn't want to believe it. Dana wanted a happy ending like in a fairy tale and couldn't understand why Bridgette didn't want the same thing. "I hate you."

"Because you know I'm right." Bridgette chuckled in response to Dana's assertion.

"Yes. And you're an asshole for letting me believe we stood a chance for so long."

"I'll accept it. I'm an asshole."

They had already kissed once that day, and the longer Dana stared at Bridgette, the more she wished she could forgive her. Although she detested Bridgette's dishonest behavior, their relationship was straightforward. Bridgette's smoldering cockiness set Dana's heart racing. She took a baby step forward to give her ex-wife a last, tender kiss before they parted ways for good.

She turned and left the office, saying nothing else. Soon, she found herself crying behind the closed elevator door.

# ANGIE

Dana added a white peony to the hand-tied bridal bouquet for the wedding that weekend. As if she were the bride, she held it in front of her waist, reflecting in the mirror back to her own nuptials. She repeatedly vowed never to get married again, but every time she held bouquets of flowers in front of her, she yearned for the happily ever after marriage bliss. She didn't think she'd find it at fifty-four years of age. The years of happily ever afters were behind her.

Dana exhaled deeply as she wrapped the stems in a double-faced champagne satin ribbon and placed them in a holding vase with some water at the bottom. Michelle entered the shop carrying a Vietnamese iced coffee precisely as she emerged from the floral cooler.

Michelle extended her hand. "I know you claim to have sworn off all women but hear me out."

She accepted her friend's coffee and drank a sip. "I don't like bribes, but this one is delicious. Thank you, and what do I need to hear?"

"This week a new girl started working at the museum, and yesterday we were chatting. She has a sister who is roughly your age—"

"You make me sound like an antiquity among your

collections." Dana abruptly cut her off.

"Whatever," Michelle continued. "Amanda is attractive, which bodes well for the sister, and she likes the ladies."

"I'm assuming you're referring to the sister, in which case you're attempting to set me up on a blind date?"

"According to Amanda, her sister has been single for about a year and hasn't really gone out. I know you despise blind dates, but haven't all your previous ones been essentially blind dates?"

Dana sat her coffee down and finished cleaning up her design station while she talked with Michelle. "True. That's fine. Just tell let me when and where you want me to be, and I'll be there."

Michelle had picked up a bucket of unused flowers, but when Dana agreed to go, she sat it down with a thump. She stood up, a puzzled expression on her face. Dana stepped out of the cooler, wide-eyed, to see Michelle. "What?"

"You're not arguing with me?" Michelle questioned.

"No." Dana shrugged, picking up the bucket in front of Michelle. "What will it hurt, really? It couldn't be any worse than what I've already been through. I almost forgave Bridgette, and if I'm willing to do that, I'm sure I can give this woman a chance."

"That's great." Michelle finished her statement after Dana went into the cooler. "You have a date tonight."

She appeared from the cooler with a twisted

expression. "Seriously? Tonight?" Dana shook her head and pinched her lips together before exaggerating her smile. "Fine. When and where?"

"Five-thirty. And at Toto's Italian."

Dana checked her fitness watch to see what time it was. "That's like in an hour. I won't have time to go home and shower. I appreciate the short notice."

"This way, you won't go home and back out." Michelle laughed and smiled.

Michelle knew her too well, especially since she hated blind dates. Plus, Dana didn't want to keep looking for her next true love. Dana would have canceled, and Michelle perceived it ahead of time. "Fine, but you owe me."

Dana closed up shop shortly after five o'clock and headed to Toto's, a restaurant close to the florist. She maneuvered her way into a parking spot as she drove in. Three police cars were blocking most of the road, and cops hovered around a man on the ground.

A small crowd gathered to watch the police show as she approached the front door. "What's going on?" Dana asked a woman next to her.

"Homeless man making a spectacle. When I got there, he was in the middle of the street trying to control the flow of traffic," the woman said.

As she walked into the restaurant, Dana prepared for the part of blind dates she detested the most: locating the date. "Hello," the waitress said, looking up from her seating diagram. "Just one tonight?"

"No. Actually, I'm meeting someone, but I'm not

sure what she looks like," Dana said, bracing herself for the pitying glance from the young, vivacious waitress who obviously had her life together.

A voice from behind her said, "Probably me. Dana?"

Dana turned around to see the woman outside, enthralled by the police show. "Amanda's sister?" she asked, smiling. "I'm sorry. That's all I've been told."

"Yes. Hi. My name is Angie. It's a pleasure to officially meet you. There's a bit of chaos out front," Angie said.

The restaurant door opened from behind Angie, and a policeman entered. Officer Morales caught Dana's attention. "Can I get a glass of water, please?" the cop pleaded as she pushed her way in front of everyone.

The hostess dashed away, and while the officer waited, she noticed Dana. "Oh, hi. By the way, my mother adored flowers."

"That's fantastic, Cynthia. I'm glad to hear it," Dana said as they waited to be seated.

Dana ignored her date while they exchanged a caring smile. "You remembered my name," Office Morales said, blushing slightly.

The hostess then returned with the water and handed it over. Cynthia Morales shuffled off and out the door, and Dana returned her attention to the hostess and her companion. The hostess asked, "So, just the two of you tonight?"

"Unless the sexy cop wants to join us for a threesome," Angie added.

Her demeanor turned Dana off immediately. Even though being gay and open about it was not a problem for Dana, she did not enjoy it when other people thrust their sexuality in other people's faces, especially when they did so in the form of comments like a threesome. Dana did not respond, but she added, "Officer Morales is a client of mine."

Angie commented as the hostess led them to their table, "Nevertheless, she's extremely hot and totally worth going to jail for if she'll put me in handcuffs."

Dana wouldn't disagree with that, nor would she agree with it. In the middle of the room, they sat down at a table. Even though it wasn't her ideal place to sit, she made the best of it. When she ate, Dana preferred to do so in secluded nooks and out of the way places, but Angie might be more subdued and less outspoken if she were in the spotlight.

Angie ordered a soda, and Dana ordered a glass of red wine for herself before they even started talking. From the way they dressed to the beverages they consumed, Dana could tell that they differed greatly from one another. Dana, very aware of what Bridgette had said about her, refrained from passing judgment on the situation too quickly. She couldn't close herself off to their disparities.

Dana chuckled as they waited for their drinks. "I'm assuming you know as much about me as I do about you. Nothing. I work as a florist. Born and raised in Tampa, but attended college here. Never left. I don't want to sound like a generic dating ad when I say I enjoy long walks on the beach, but I do."

The two of them shared a laugh as the waiter returned with their drinks. Dana drank from her wineglass as Angie removed her straw from its packaging. Angie reached for a piece of bread, bit into it, and then, after a few chews, she remarked, "A florist sounds interesting. I grew up in Tampa, too. Actually, in Brandon, but isn't that really just another part of Tampa?"

Dana's eyes widened. "Me too. Where did you go to high school?"

"Brandon High, of course."

Dana smiled. "What year?"

"Class of eight-six."

"I was eight-five. We would have been there at the same time. That's such a coincidence." The realization Dana and this other woman shared a connection brought a warm feeling to Dana's heart. They could reminisce about teachers and form a friendship of sorts.

Angie added, "My ex-wife graduated from there in eighty-six too."

"What was her name?"

"Stella Heller."

"Stell from Hell," Dana exclaimed, laughing. "Oh, my goodness. That's insane. We were in a band together. I had no idea she was gay, or that she turned out to be a lesbian. I'd ask how she's doing, but you're divorced."

"Very much. And in high school, she was very much a lesbian, but she didn't come out until much later in life. Me? They ostracized me for being too gay.

Almost every week, I got into fights over it."

Dana covered her mouth with her hand as she remembered a tough girl at school who everyone called a dyke. "I'm pretty sure I remember you. A tom-girl who wore a leather jacket?"

"Yup. That was me."

"Wow. This is hilarious. Who would have thought a blind date wouldn't be so blind? So, tell me, what do you do now?" Dana asked, relaxing into the conversation.

After placing their food orders, they carried on their conversation. Angie described her life after divorce. "I'm now a certified travel agent with a few people working for me. I hadn't worked in so long that I needed to find something to do to make some money after my divorce."

Dana raised an eyebrow at Angie and inquired, "Is there a big market for travel agents? I'd think that with the internet, everyone just goes direct now."

"Yes. You can make a lot of money doing it. As I said, I have a few people working for me and am looking to hire more. The more people I recruit for my agency, the more money I make with percentages."

When Angie described the job, it sounded more like a pyramid scheme than anything else. Dana listened without being judgmental in the way Bridgette insisted she could be when she disagreed.

Angie continued, "As a florist, you assist people with their weddings. You should seriously consider getting certified. It doesn't take much effort, but you could ask people where they intend on spending their honeymoon, and it wouldn't be difficult at all to book those trips."

Dana nodded.

"I could sign you up with my agency, and in a short amount of time, you could work your way up to the bronze or even gold status. It only takes a few successful bookings for you to launch your own travel agency. Make even more money."

This pattern lasted for a good part of the evening. Angie discussed travel and the destinations she hoped to visit once she attained gold status and received a free trip somewhere. Dana attempted to change the subject, hoping to find another topic the two of them shared in common other than their high school. Angie mentioned more than once she preferred not to discuss it because it brought back too many unpleasant memories.

Finally, when the waiter brought the check, Dana pulled out her wallet while Angie took the check in her hand. She looked it over and started going through each line to determine who ordered what. Angie went so far as to request a menu once more in order to determine whether the waiter overcharged them. Dana nodded and handed the credit card to the man while Angie looked the check over with critical eyes.

"Angie, don't worry about it," Dana told Angie as the waiter returned with a second copy of the bill. "It's my pleasure. I took care of it."

Angie argued. "Why? I just figured everything out. How can you be sure that they didn't overcharge you?"

"No worries. Really. It's fine." Dana waved her

away, signed her name, and then tripled the tip Angie had planned to leave. A yawn emerged from her mouth after a phony stretch of her arms. Dana said, "I'm sorry I need to call an end to this night. It has been quite a long day and I have a wedding to set up in the morning."

"No worries. You should look into the entire travel industry. I believe you have the potential to be a one-stop shop for brides. If you're interested, let me know, and I'll send you a video explaining how it all works," Angie said, returning to the subject of travel.

"I'll consider it." Dana stood up and sipped her last swig of wine. "It's been a pleasant evening. Thank you very much."

They exited together. Dana took larger strides to her car, whereas Angie walked in the opposite direction of the parking lot. Just as Dana was about to slide into her front seat, Angie yelled, "I forgot to give you my number!"

Dana entered her car without hesitation, and as she shut the door, she said to herself, "It's definitely okay. I wouldn't have called you, anyway."

Dana pulled out and drove away. She called Michelle about halfway down the street and recounted the evening's events in play-by-play fashion. Even her closest friend agreed she should back off from a romantic connection with Angie. It would be best for her to keep her distance from any schemes involving making money.

Michelle asked, "So what now?"

Dana let out a long sigh. "You know. Perhaps I'm

doomed to be single for the rest of my life. I could buy a ranch and turn into a crazy cat lady with a shitload of them."

"I'm sorry it didn't work out, but I don't think I like the idea of a cat farm. I adore Jinx, but I think one cat is enough for me."

# JOSIE

*Hello, my name is Josie! I'm a proud dog owner and a regular gym-goer. My friends say I'm sometimes a bit strange. I'm looking for a woman who will improve my life and is eager to try everything this world has to offer.*

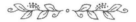

**P**icky. Not picky. On a Friday evening, Dana found herself alone and able to relax at home. Michelle had a date. Scott had two. Her designer Miguel had a live-in boyfriend. Being by oneself could bring about a sense of great solace. Dana didn't have to explain herself to anyone about what she did. Nobody would say anything negative about it if she wanted to eat Mexican food for two nights in a row.

While the benefits of being single were plentiful, she didn't realize how much she'd missed having someone else around until her friends forced her to date. The Pryde dating app had matched her with people she remembered swiping left to dismiss. It's possible she combed through every single record in their database. That was one of the many reasons

Dana deleted it, but she wasn't ready to end her search, especially after witnessing Bridgette on a date with none other than Tiffany, the woman who loved strippers.

She searched the internet for additional dating services and eventually joined one, which offered a great deal more variety than Pryde did in its membership options. Cvrves. After completing the setup process, Dana received a match with a compatibility rating of ninety-six percent. The fact the algorithm ranked people rather than simply displaying a profile was something that appealed to her.

Dana combed over Josie's profile in great detail, looking for anything that seemed out of the ordinary. Everything appeared fine except for a few acronyms she overlooked. The woman's eyes were the clearest shade of green, and her hair was a light blonde color, about shoulder length with a touch of a wave. Dana gave a casual shrug and clicked the heart button, which brought up a screen where she could communicate with the potential match.

She tapped out a standard greeting and mentioned the system's high compatibility rating, joking the computer might be smarter than she was at picking a match for herself. She waited for a reply while exploring the app to find more highly rated matches.

It took about an hour for Josie to respond, and her message included a phone number so that they could talk to each other directly. When Dana called, a seductively deep voice picked up the phone. Dana wanted to learn more about the woman before agreeing to meet her, so the two of them had a lengthy conversation over the phone. The call ended with both parties expressing a desire to advance to the next level. Because of the crazy people online, Josie suggested they should meet at a neutral location. Dana mentioned a late night bistro that evening or the following day. When Josie agreed to meet that same night, Dana got ready and headed to the restaurant.

Dana found herself a seat at an outdoor table. It was easier to greet people outside, where the atmosphere was slightly less awkward. There wasn't much of a wait as Josie approached, wearing a cute outfit Dana could easily picture herself wearing. Dana stood up as they exchanged greetings. It was the first time she ever gave praise to a potential date. "That blouse is stunning. It looks fantastic on you."

"Thank you," Josie replied, her voice husky. "That makes me feel so validated."

"Well, let's get something to drink and then we can come back out to the patio, unless you prefer to sit inside," Dana offered while holding the door open for Josie.

"The patio is perfect. It's such a lovely evening. It's not too humid, which is great. I despise the humidity. It gives me such curls." Josie tapped her hair, ensuring it wasn't out of place.

They walked together to the counter. Dana placed her order, then asked, "What would you like? I'm going to buy."

"Thank you very much. You're such a sweetie."

Josie took a moment to find a drink before placing her order. "Do you live around here?" Josie asked as they moved aside. Just as Dana opened her mouth, Josie chuckled. "No. I'm sorry. Don't say. I could be a serial killer."

Dana laughed with Josie. "I doubt you are, but wise idea. I've had some real numbers I've gone out with. How long have you been using this dating site?"

"Not for long. I was expecting a swarm of creepers, but there you were." Josie then leaned forward, her voice quiet and her eyes wild. "Unless you are the serial killer?"

It was the second time Josie mentioned the murderous act, and it took Dana completely by surprise both times. She hoped the date would go swimmingly, but things headed south even before they had coffee.

Josie continued by saying, "You know, it's impossible to get to know people completely. According to what I've read, most murderers are people who appear perfectly normal. As if there wasn't anything peculiar or out of the ordinary about them."

When the barista put Dana's drink down on the counter, Dana reached for it, then picked up Josie's drink and passed it to her. "Well, I can tell you without a shadow of a doubt that I've never killed anyone, and I don't plan on starting with you."

Josie let out a hearty guffaw with her distinctively rough and low-pitched voice. Dana expected Josie to return the statement, but she didn't; instead, she turned on her heel and walked to the door. Dana followed.

Dana heard Josie's phone chime as they left the café, and as soon as they sat down, Josie took it out of her purse and read the message. She started tapping on the screen, clearly in response to a message sent to her.

It didn't register with Dana as particularly significant until Josie said, "Another woman from the website. I figured I would have a contingency plan if things didn't work out. A girl can't be too picky, can she?"

It was a strange topic to bring up on a date or during a meeting while on another one. Dana attempted to not make any snap conclusions about Josie based on her eccentricities. She sat back in her wrought-iron chair and made herself comfortable so that she could respond to Josie's oncoming barrage of questions.

The questions were typical of those asked on a first date, and Dana responded to them with ease. One after the other, with not much of a pause in between, Josie did not give Dana the opportunity to ask questions back to her.

Dana did not mind being the center of attention until Josie asked, "What is your opinion on livestock?"

She suppressed a cough and refrained from spitting out her coffee. Dana whispered, "Pardon me?"

Josie lowered her voice and held up her hand. "I apologize. It's way too early to get personal. It's your turn; get to know me beforehand."

Dana shifted in her chair, straightening her backbone, and sitting more upright. "No. Uh. What exactly did you mean?"

Josie leaned in and lowered her voice so others could not hear. "Drinking animal blood? I know most people gravitate toward human, but I have a soft spot for pigs."

Dana's mouth dropped open in shock because she had not been expecting Josie to say such a thing. Josie recoiled in her seat and covered her mouth in response to Dana's expression. The other's mannerisms took aback both of them. Dana brought her fingers close to her mouth as she searched for the right words to say.

Josie leaned back in her chair, running her fingers through her hair, breaking the awkward silence. "I was under the impression you had a similar kink. Please accept my apologies. So, tell me, what's your vibe?"

"I guess I'm not up on what things mean," Dana said slowly and precisely. "What exactly do you mean by vibe?"

Josie smiled. "Your kink, honey. Why did you message me if you're not interested in RSIV?"

She swallowed forcefully, but the knot in her throat refused to dissolve. Dana's shoulders cocked, suggesting she was in over her head. "RSIV? There's no kink. I thought you were pretty."

"Thank you. I don't hear that very often, but darling, I'm not into MTF fetishes, so if that's what this is, I'm out."

"Pardon me? Fetishes?" Again, Dana found herself extremely out of her element. "I clearly don't understand what we're talking about here. I'm not a fetishist."

"Then why are you vag-hunting on Cvrves?"

Dana sat back in her chair. "There is clearly a misunderstanding. I'm completely lost."

"Baby, do you know what Cvrves is?"

"Perhaps I don't." Dana cocked her head, waiting for Josie to explain yet another trend she had completely misidentified.

"It's a dating site for kink. What did you think you joined?"

Dana laughed, her cheeks turning a deep crimson. "I assumed it was for more mature, curvy people."

"Chubbies?" Josie extended her hand across the table. Her large, solid hands encased hers. Josie continued, "You know, chubby chasers are a kink."

Dana finally understood that Josie was a trans woman. She couldn't stop laughing and realized she was more connected to Josie than ever before, albeit on a different level. "Well, I totally feel like a boomer, and I'm so sorry I'm a fool. Please forgive me for misleading you about the date because I'm feeling the shame for both of us here."

"Don't worry, doll. I'm just relieved I didn't have to dump your ass out of gender kink. You have no idea how big of a deal that is."

While Dana still had a great deal of confusion regarding the pig blood incident, she expressed her sadness for the woman, who explained that she experienced many psychopaths were interested in dating her because of her transitioning status. "And that is why I took MTF off my profile," Josie confirmed.

"That makes perfect sense. I stand by my statement that you are extremely attractive, and I still adore your outfit. Thank you for being understanding about my blunder. I'm going to delete my profile and probably stop online dating."

Both of them finished their coffees and then enjoyed the evening together on a non-date. By the time they called it a night, the two of them became friends. It's possible Dana made a mistake, but in the end, Josie was a charming woman who liked her blood and wanted to drink it too.

# TAYLOR

*48. I'm looking for friends, lovers, and partners. I
need a deep and meaningful connection, but I'd rather
it happen slowly. My personality is lively and eccentric.
It's fun for me to get to know new people through their
spirituality and experiences with other people.*

D ana needed to get ready for her busy
season, which would incorporate a lot
of pine and misted sapphire greens with
shimmery glitter on it, as the early fall season
approached. The annual market was a staple of the
industry, where florists and interior decorators can
discover innovative products and get a sneak peek at
next year's offerings. A place where Dana typically
planned her new line of gifts and merchandise for the
coming year while also buying her holiday containers.

After joining a fetish app in a misguided
attempt to avoid competing with super models and
cosmetically enhanced people, she swore off dating.
She repainted her townhouse now that she had more
time on her hands, and she also focused on herself by

going outside on the weekends and spending time in nature.

Since the flower shop required her undivided attention, she closed the store for the week and headed to the industry convention out of town. After landing in Atlanta, she checked into her hotel and immediately went to a networking event hosted by one of the major floral committees.

She was not a fan of the social cocktail hours, but she enjoyed getting to know other florists from different parts of the country. They struck her as an eclectic bunch of oddballs, each with their own peculiarities. There was so much knowledge to be gained from everyone, including shop owners and floral designers. What might work in New York might not always translate well to Orlando, but Dana could take bits and pieces and mold it into her own style.

There were not a great number of lesbians working in the floral industry. It was extremely difficult to find another one in the sea of gay men and straight mommies who flocked to the convention. Dana was friendly and approachable, but every once in a while she wished she could find someone else just like her.

During the networking social, Dana gravitated toward a group of flamboyant designers who were laughing at how awful the new floral trend colors were for the upcoming season. She stayed at a distance and listened to their never-ending complaining about how the eighties neon returned in abundance. She finally laughed out loud, at which point they invited her to join their inner circle.

Following a considerable amount of idle chatter, the group eventually dispersed, leaving Dana with a male married couple. Discussion shifted from business to something more personal. When they asked her where her significant other was, Dana could only respond, "Not extremely significant when she's out chasing everything in a skirt."

After a tirade against her ex-wife, the men revealed they had hooked up through an online social platform that also included a dating component. It wasn't really a place to look for one-night stands. Potential partners linked with daily-used person profiles thanks to its integration with social media.

This feature was unknown to Dana, so it piqued her curiosity. Therefore, when she returned to her hotel room, the first thing she did was look up the titillating section of the website, then created a profile for the dating function. She entered her information and her areas of interest, and after a few moments, a list of prospective candidates appeared on the screen in front of her.

Again, Dana used her finger to swipe away the people who failed to pique her interest, but stopped at a woman who had stunning eyes. Exactly how the guys described it, Dana clicked the button to view the woman's profile and cast an inquisitive eye over her everyday activities. Seeing someone engaged in the community by commenting and liking posts was a welcomed sight. She scrolled through the woman's personal photographs and discovered her life wasn't just a three hundred word synopsis filled with a few hidden secrets.

She navigated back to the dating section with the click of a button and read Taylor's opening statement once more. Meaningful connections. Slowly evolving. Spiritual experiences. Was this chick for real?

Without a doubt, she was. Taylor joined the dating site three months ago, but her profile said she had been a member for years. She had to be everything, including the proverbial bag of chips. Dana felt compelled to send her a message immediately, thinking perhaps they could meet when she returned to Orlando. It gave Dana an entire week to talk with the woman and get a sense of the eccentric personality she possessed.

Dana loved the connection between the social media aspect and the dating app. It allowed her to spot when users were online. And chatting took place right next to other conversations with friends and family. Dana didn't obsess over Taylor's whereabouts, but the platform notified her when Taylor logged on while Dana chatted with her mother.

Dana received a message from Taylor in a matter of seconds. Dana's face suddenly broke out in a broad grin. As had been the case every other time, she exuded a sense of optimism as soon as she read the first message. These initial conversations with someone became almost ritualistic for her. Dana's heart raced with excitement at the prospect of meeting someone new.

After a few back-and-forth messages, Taylor

finally asked if they could share a video feed because she preferred to talk instead of typing out her responses. Dana agreed because she detested messaging as well. The screen flickered and both video feeds appeared side by side.

Taylor's warm smile and bright eyes greeted Dana, who smiled passively, like a girl with a high school crush. Dana's voice shook as she asked, "How is your evening going so far?"

"A little dull. Trying to get a few household chores done so they don't pile up and require an entire day of scrubbing," Taylor replied. Her voice was light, subtle, and soothing. She didn't rush through her words. They simply flowed like water from a faucet.

By osmosis, Taylor's slowness calmed Dana's naturally hurried words. Dana felt more at ease when they talked about life instead of relationships. "I understand how you feel. Things just fall into place if I do a bit every day. Unlike my friends, who can't go out because they always need to clean."

Taylor fixed her gaze on the camera. Her fingers rubbed over her lips as she studied Dana's screen. "I'm delighted you messaged me. I apologize for briefly stalking your profile before responding. You're a florist? That's pretty intriguing. I don't believe I've ever met one."

Dana chuckled slightly. "I actually hear that quite often. Even though there are so many flower shops in the country, nobody seems to know a florist by name."

"You like your job?" Taylor asked.

"It's fantastic. I don't consider it a job because it's

enjoyable to transform a collection of small blooms into something beautiful."

The two women went ahead with their leisurely, but increasingly methodical, conversation. Taylor didn't ask Dana a series of leading questions, but she crafted a highly deliberate way to draw out the conversation. As the evening progressed, Dana became increasingly aware of her forwardness, but she did not find it offensive in the least.

"You know," Dana said when she realized the time. "I'm in Atlanta on business, and I have to get up early tomorrow. If you're interested, I'd like to meet up with you when I get back next week."

Taylor smiled and nodded. "However, before we agree to that, I'd like to state that I am bisexual and believe in ethical non-monogamy."

Dana tilted her head, unsure whether she should go on. Dana reiterated what Taylor said. "Does that mean an open relationship with both men and women?"

"I get the impression you are not interested in that. It's not that I'm trying to hide it on the dating site; it's just there are so many unicorn-hunters, and I don't need that in my life. Therefore, I vet people before and share my preferences afterwards. The world is full of insane people. I know you said you need to get going, but I wanted to tell you this before we ended the chat. I'm absolutely interested in getting to know you more, if you are open to my type of lifestyle."

Dana wanted to be honest with Taylor. She needed

to look within herself to see if that was something she could live with or not. "I'm not saying no, but I need a little of time to process. I've never had an open relationship, so I'm unsure of how I feel about them."

"Honest enough. Think about it and please, get some sleep for the both of us."

And that settled it. Dana bid farewell and ended the call. She would have to carefully weigh the pros and cons of an open relationship with a woman who obviously liked men.

Dana took off her shoes as soon as she got back to the hotel after a long day of walking the halls of the convention center. She unloaded the stack of pamphlets and business cards and organized them by subject. Vases. Gifts. Gourmet items. Store decor.

As she rested in her bed, she scrolled through her feed and saw a photo of Taylor next to a swimming pool wearing an adorable sun hat. Dana could not deny Taylor was cute. With her smile, Taylor was just as seductive as Bridgette, who could have any woman she wanted. Taylor also had a certain sweetness about her.

Dana read the comments in which Taylor instructed someone to view her photos on her other social media account. Dana's business used the other platform, but she herself did not. She logged in and conducted a quick search to locate Taylor's page, where she scrolled through pages of photos. Some with female friends and others with a male companion. That same male companion with whom

Taylor cuddled up to him.

When Dana clicked on the photos and read the description, she discovered Taylor had a profound sexual soul. Most of the text beneath the photographs consisted of poems and short stories with graphic language. Dana wondered if these were actual events or merely the attention-seeking ramblings of a sex-craved woman. In any case, the text generated a strange sense of attraction towards this woman. And although Dana was not one to share, the idea of pleasing this beautiful woman sounded both amazing and challenging.

Dana sat on her hotel room's balcony, regarding the city and its congestion of traffic. With her phone in hand, she opened the chat window and sent Taylor a message. *What does an open relationship with you look like?*

After only a few seconds, a request for a video chat requested Dana to join. When she clicked accept, Taylor appeared on her screen, looking just as beautiful as she had the night before.

With no hello or formal welcome, Taylor replied, "I go out and have a good time whenever and with whomever I choose. If everyone agrees with the arrangement, there is no conflict. There is a man in my life with whom I have mutual respect. He cannot satisfy all my needs. I cannot fulfill all his needs. We have an ethical, non-monogamous relationship for this reason. Even though we aren't married, he lives with me. My need to be in a relationship with a woman is the one aspect of my life he cannot fulfill for me. My girlfriend decided about a year ago she wanted more. More than I could give her."

"What couldn't you give her?" Dana asked.

"A wife."

"Was the relationship of the threesome kind?"

"No. My two worlds may intersect, but they do not entwine unless it is mutual. She was uninterested in men, and I'm assuming you are, as well."

"I'm very much a lesbian. Not that I have nothing against bisexuality or group sex; I'm just not that kind of person. Me and guys will never mix."

"Fair enough. And I'd never ask. I'm surprised to hear from you again. Perhaps I should have given you more credit; I pictured you running for the hills."

Dana laughed from the depths of her stomach. "I would be lying if I said I hadn't considered it. My wife — excuse me, ex-wife — cheated on me multiple times, which is what led to our divorce, so this whole open relationship is a," Dana paused and said, "new thing."

"Here is where ethical considerations come into play. I do not consider it cheating if you are aware, and will accept the possibility that I will have sexual relations with other people."

"Are you only looking to be with one man and one woman? Or do you have multiple males and females?" Dana asked, still attempting to comprehend where she would fall if she accepted Taylor's lifestyle.

"Mark and I have been members of a swinger's club for some time. I am largely satisfied with my male and female partners, but there are nights when you just want a little spice. We will go out and meet other couples. Dana, I am an extremely sexual person. I don't want to lie and say that if you and I were to get together, I wouldn't want to feel another woman on my skin."

Dana shrugged her shoulders and remained silent before speaking. She pondered whether she could be content with a woman who slept with others, especially when she couldn't accept when Bridgette did so.

When Dana didn't respond, Taylor asked, "So, did I scare you away yet?"

Dana exhibited a measure of backbone and cockiness occasionally. She gave a smirk before responding with her own question. "Did I close the video feed?"

"Okay. So." Taylor's eyes flashed with a flirtatious teasing that contained an undercurrent of a dare as they gazed at her. "Now that I have your attention, tell me about the qualities that are most important to you in a romantic partner."

If Dana placed her hope in Taylor for the future, everything Dana desired became largely unimportant. If she wanted to date Taylor, she would have to abandon the idea of having a committed partner. Since Taylor already lived with Mark, it was unlikely the two of them would decide to move in together. Dana remarked, "Someone who wants to go out for drinks and dinner. Come home and make passionate love. A person who genuinely loves me and believes in me. I really do not know. Someone to love?"

Whatever the lighting, Taylor's eyes glistened. As she spoke, the corners of her mouth turned upward as she said, "And all of that is available to you if you would like to give this a shot. After last night, I was really hoping to hear from you, and you're here. It's possible the constellations have finally aligned in our favor."

Dana added a little caveat. "What I mean to say is this. At the moment, I do not have a problem with the whole open relationship thing, but I want to clarify that while I am gone, I reserve the right to come to a different conclusion."

Taylor's warm expression and sympathetic eyes won Dana over once more. "I think you've come up with an excellent strategy. When you return, please contact me and we will reevaluate your decision."

"Will do. Sleep well, Taylor." Then they ended the video call, giving Dana a chance to exhale all her pesky morals that had been keeping her single.

As soon as Dana placed her bag on the counter in her kitchen after the long trip to Atlanta and back, Mr. Jinx gave her a friendly head butt to greet her. He purred as she leaned in closer to give him a kiss on the head. Because no one else was there to greet her, the empty house had an unwelcoming atmosphere. In the years before her divorce, Bridgette always greeted with a warm embrace whenever she returned home from a work trip. She also would have taken her dirty clothes and had them in the washing machine before Dana could take off her shoes.

A dagger filled with melancholy thrusted through her chest, triggering Dana as she allowed herself to dwell on the idea of no one waiting for her at home after her week-long outing.

Instead of being greeted by a loving hug, Dana reached for her phone and texted Taylor. *Just arrived home. Hope you had a good day.*

That had been Dana's life since meeting Taylor. They communicated with one another in the mornings by sending a message with a "rise and shine" greeting in it. And as the evening progressed, it continued with well wishes for restful sleep. It was charming to have such closeness with someone, but also disconcerting to return to an empty home.

Dana made her way back to the kitchen, where she opened the door to the refrigerator after she finished unpacking and putting her clothes in the wash. The sudden rush of coolness felt nice, but that there was nothing edible in it was a letdown. She knew she needed to dash out and grab a bite to eat. Because Dana felt some strange sense of accountability to Taylor already, she sent another message to her. *No food in the house. Must go out and find some sustenance.*

The moment she closed the car door, her phone chimed to alert her to a new message. *Want company?*

She had done nothing to get herself ready for the first in person meeting. Dana wanted to agree, but when she looked in the mirror and saw her sloppy appearance, she couldn't bring herself to say yes. She definitely wore a day of travel all over her.

Dana typed. *Tempting, but I look like shit.*

She started her car and slowly backed out of the parking spot. Dana's phone started ringing just as she left her complex. When she switched the phone to her car's radio, Taylor's heavenly voice reverberated throughout the entire vehicle. "I seriously doubt you look like shit. And besides, unless you changed your mind, I'll be seeing you at your worst because no one really looks good when they're being fucked."

Dana restrained herself from laughing by pursing her lips while she found Taylor's remark amusing. "That's true. I just wanted to look good when we met for the first time. And no, I haven't changed my mind."

Dana and Taylor had been messaging back and forth with each other over the course of the past few days. The open relationship might be a touchy subject, so Dana made a solemn vow to herself that she would conceal Taylor from her friends until the two of them established a solid relationship. Even though it went against everything she believed in, she couldn't help but want to be part of Taylor's world. There was something about her that intrigued Dana.

"Where are you headed to eat?" Taylor asked.

"Honestly, I have no clue. I'm just driving right now with no destination in mind because you called."

"I'd say let's meet up at this lovely Italian place off the four and four-eighty-two, but since you look like shit," Taylor laughed but continued, "Let's hit the Olive Garden."

"Sounds like you want Italian. Fine. Let's do it and hopefully I won't scare you away when you see this dirty, wayward traveler."

Dana heard the grin in Taylor's voice. "Maybe I like dirty girls."

They ended the call, and Dana made a U-turn at the intersection to continue in the opposite direction she had been going. The unabashed and uninhibited sexuality Taylor possessed was one factor that contributed to Dana's attraction to her. While Bridgette's obvious addiction to other women caused the downfall of their marriage, Taylor's sexual assurance excited Dana.

Dana waited for Taylor in the parking lot. She did

not know what kind of car she drove, so every vehicle that pulled up caught her attention. A sedan pulled up next to her, and inside the vehicle was a very familiar person. As soon as Taylor emerged from the vehicle, Dana felt a surge of self-confidence rise within herself.

Taylor walked up to her. After only seeing Taylor's face in photos and on video chats, Dana took in the rest of her body with much adoration. Taylor looked fantastic in the pair of jeans that clung to the few extra pounds she wore on her hips. Her delicate femininity shone through with each stride she took. Taylor was a confident woman who walked with her head held high and her shoulders back.

Taylor extended her hand, giving Dana's plain black shirt a light tug while flashing a cocked grin when they were finally face to face. "You do not look like shit. Trust me."

While Taylor's hand remained on her, Dana attempted to control the trembling spreading throughout her body and hoped it wouldn't be obvious that Taylor made her anxious. A lump in her throat cause her voice to crake while attempting to say, "Thank you."

They walked toward to restaurant. Dana noticed her masculine demeanor slipping out as she walked next to Taylor. The same thing happened with Bridgette as well. Dana greeted Taylor with chivalry at the door by opening it for her and allowing her to enter first.

The hostess asked, as they walked to the podium, "Table for two?"

Again, Dana allowed Taylor to take the lead, and when they reached the booth, they sat opposite one another. Because they had already spent a few days getting to know each other, the awkwardness of breaking the ice with trivial pleasantries was unnecessary.

As if they were old pals, Taylor asked, "How was the trip? And the return flight?"

"The trip turned out to be quite fruitful. Over the next few weeks, a bunch of shipments will arrive. This excites me because it brings out my creative juices. As for the flight..." Dana shrugged. "...it was what it was. Crowded. Hot."

Even though Dana spent most of the conversation listening and assessing all of Taylor's quirks and features, photos always hid, the conversation between the two of them continued without a hitch. Dana saw nothing wrong with Taylor except the fact she would return home and sleep with a man.

The dinner lasted longer than expected, with nearly three hours spent in the booth. Dana had no other obligations, so she did not rush their time together. Having someone smart, intelligent, and interesting made Taylor even more of a keeper.

When they finally gave their waiter a break and left, Dana walked Taylor to the driver's side of her car. Dana requested Taylor wait before entering the car because a family had just pulled up in front of them. Taylor's wink spoke a non-verbal understanding.

Once free from prying eyes, Dana asked, "Now

that the children and parents are safely in the restaurant, may I give you a goodbye kiss?"

"I admire your respect for others. I'd love to kiss you," Taylor agreed.

They were nearly the same height, so Dana leaned into a perfectly fluid kiss. As they parted, she bowed her head and glanced at her hands, which fiddled with the front of Taylor's shirt. While it didn't embarrass Dana to kiss her, she doubted herself on if it was even good enough. In terms of the number of partners, Dana's adventures paled in comparison to those of Taylor.

Taylor cocked her head to meet Dana's gaze. "Are you rethinking your decision?"

"No. Not at all. I really want to kiss you again." When the words rushed out of her mouth, Dana's gaze ascended.

A giggle paved the way for Taylor to lean in for a second, significantly deeper kiss. More passionate than the first soft and sweet one. Dana nearly lost her breath in response. As Taylor pulled away, Dana pushed forward and eventually assumed control of the third.

Taylor said as the kiss ended with only an inch separating them. "Good, because I really enjoy kissing you." She stroked Dana's face while saying, "I should leave. I'm sure you're tired. And if I continue to kiss you, I may not want to leave."

Taylor opened the door to her car, and Dana moved aside to let her in. Dana leaned through the gap and said, "Thank you for insisting on dinner."

Before Dana closed the door for Taylor, the two of them exchanged a gaze that was both persistent and longing. With a wave, she moved out of the way so Taylor could leave. Dana took a deep breath out of her chest and expelled it slowly as she reflected on the events of the evening and where the relationship could go. The thing she couldn't wrap her head around was how simple it was to get into bed with Cheryl and even have Aladdin sex with Mya. Those two weren't even as lovely as Taylor. Yet here was a woman who exuded sexuality, and Dana was alone, masturbating herself to sleep.

There hadn't been a single day in which Dana and Taylor hadn't either spoken or messaged one another. And as time went on, the two of them became closer, which led to a beautiful friendship. Their lack of face-to-face contact was attributable to their respective hectic work schedules. Dates were difficult to coordinate, but despite her frustration, Dana understood. Work was necessary for people to survive.

Dana sat at her desk and rubbed her lips together, remembering the last time she and Taylor kissed. It had been about three weeks. Even though she wasn't particularly thinking about Taylor at that moment, she longed for the gentle touch of a pair of hands on her. As the shop's front door opened, the cowbell clucked. Dana jumped down from her seat, whirled around the wall, then stopped in the middle of a step when she reached the floor of the showroom. "Taylor?"

"Is that a good or bad tone in your voice? Should I leave?" Taylor asked, pointing out the door.

Other than expressing surprise, Dana's tone might not had shown her excitement. She laughed as she shook her head in response. "Good, of course. I'm just surprised to see you."

"That's the whole point of surprises as long as there's no bad intentions involved."

"In terms of seeing you, this is a welcoming surprise, one that I'll take any day." Dana's eyes widened as her mind chased back to how unlucky in love she was. "Please don't say you came to see me because you needed some flowers for someone else."

"No one else. Mark doesn't like them. Therefore, I came for you. I was in the neighborhood. Just finished with a customer around the corner. I figured I'd stop in and see my favorite person." As she spoke, Taylor's angelic voice immediately eased any tension or wrong speculations that may have been present. Taylor had that effect on her. Her voice never wavered from its gentle and reassuring quality. She had a trace of a southern accent in her speech, which Dana found humble.

Quite the opposite of Dana's straightforwardness, and lack of pleasantries. She ignored the favorite comment, more so because she hated gushing over people. "Let me show you around the shop. It's almost like a second home to me."

They went on a quick tour, which culminated in a visit to Dana's office. She extended an offer of a seat to her, but she did not move out of the way for Taylor to really enter the office. A shot of adrenaline in the chest surged through Dana, which gave her the boost of courage she needed to press her lips against Taylor's without asking. After the amazing conversations they had and intense flirting via video chats, Dana wouldn't ask for permission again. Taylor gently pressed her finger over Dana's mouth as soon as they parted. "I like this more confident version of you."

And at that very second, the sexual energy between them reached a fever pitch. Dana roused the daring spirit that slept deep within her and prepared to throw this woman onto her desk. The door chimed and opened just as Dana's hands took hold of Taylor's waist and their lips touched.

"It's me." Miguel's voice reverberated throughout the shop.

The two women shared a wry smile, and both sighed heavily with a chuckle. "My employee." Dana took a few steps back and flashed another grin.

"Slow burn, my love," Taylor said as she walked out of the office behind Dana.

When they stepped out of the little cubby of an office, Miguel flashed an arrogant grin with his brow raised. "Oh. You've got company."

Dana understood exactly what Miguel meant as he looked at the flush in her cheeks. "This is Taylor. Taylor, this is Miguel."

Taylor said, "Nice to meet you," in a soft but casual voice. She addressed Dana next. "I need to get going. I just wanted to stop by and say hello."

It's possible there would have been more if Miguel hadn't returned from lunch at that precise moment. Deflated, Dana escorted Taylor to her vehicle. They stood at the driver's side door. Again, Dana fiddled with the front of Taylor's shirt at the waist, but this time she consciously tried to hide her anxiety. Even after many lengthy conversations with Taylor, Dana couldn't figure out why this woman heightened her shyness.

"You and I will have to make some time together," Taylor remarked as she reached out and took Dana's hand.

"This weekend?" Dana turned her gaze upward with anticipation in her eyes.

"Saturday is my day off."

"Dinner?"

"If you're up to it, I have something even better than that."

"What is it?"

"Some friends invited me to go to this club this weekend. It's an exclusive lifestyle club. If you want to come with me, it might be fun."

Dana's eyebrows arched with curiosity. "What exactly is a lifestyle club?"

She didn't answer immediately, though her eyes said more than enough. Dana could only imagine. Taylor stated, "The name of the club is Flourdelis North, a play on words similar to a fleur-de-lis. They have a website. Research it and decide if you want to come with me. I'll pay for your entry if you say yes."

"Okay. I'll look it up," Dana said, without supplying an answer to her question.

After whisking her hand across Dana's cheek, she leaned in and gave her a gentle kiss before slipping into her vehicle and driving away. Dana shook her head as she stood in the parking lot, shocked she had even considered dating a sexually promiscuous woman.

She walked back into her shop. Miguel said, "Ay, que rica" as soon as she appeared in the design room. "That is one spicy tamale."

"Yes, she is." Dana heaved a sigh as she shut the door to her office and spent the rest of the afternoon researching the club's online presence by visiting their website and checking out their various social media accounts.

The club promoted itself as a consortium for those with an inquisitive nature. On the website of this female-friendly club, they stated male patrons could only enter the establishment if a female guest accompanied them, but women were free to go there on their own. Although they did not serve alcohol, guests were welcome to bring their own alcoholic beverages to consume on the premises. They wanted their guests to visit, relax, dance, have a drink, be alone with their significant other, engage in conversation with other people, and socialize with like-minded friends. The guests had the choice of being a voyeur or exhibitionist. And if one felt courageous, they could join a group of people willing to engage in intimate relationships.

There was no direct mention of sex on the website, though when Dana read the section that addressed frequently asked questions, it stated possibilities for sexual activity happened on the premises. Participation was not mandatory. Dana stared blankly at an advertisement on the website, which featured an old photograph that looked like an oil painting of an orgy. Her eyes blinked as her mind whirled over the picture. A scenario ran through her head of Taylor having sexual intercourse with several other people while she stood on the sidelines and watched.

***What are you wearing to this club on Saturday?*** Dana messaged Taylor just as she got home from work. She did chores around the house, including throwing a load of laundry into the washing machine and giving the toilet a speedy scrub. Dana was in the midst of cooking a quick stir-fry when her phone rang. As soon as she saw Taylor's name pop up on her screen, she picked up the phone and cradled it in the bend of her neck.

"Theme is naughty schoolgirls. I'm going to leave that up to your imagination for the time being. Have you decided to come?" Taylor prompted.

While Dana stirred her vegetables in the pan, she declared, "One thing is for certain: I will not be dressing like a schoolgirl."

"I wouldn't expect you to, even though I could picture you as a stern teacher holding a wooden ruler, prepared to use it," she said. The tone of Taylor's voice held an undercurrent of teasing.

"I didn't think you were interested in that," Dana said, recalling they previously discussed how Taylor hadn't interacted with anyone who belonged to the kinky BDSM world.

"If you were the one in charge of the ruler, I might consider playing along." There was no denying it. Taylor was a tease. Not receiving a reply from Dana, she continued, "Does the thought of that frighten you or excite you?"

Dana pushed the pan away from the flame and leaned against the counter as her heart raced. As she spoke those words, Dana's voice dropped slightly as she emphasized each word. "Everything about you excites me."

Taylor's voice volume matched that of Dana's. "Is it safe to assume that this Saturday we'll be spending time together?"

She couldn't remember the last time she could flirt with another person; it had been an exceedingly long time. Dana said to her, "If that's the only way I get to see you dressed as a schoolgirl, then I'll take it."

"A naughty schoolgirl."

Dana imagined the scene in her mind, and as she did, the word *fuck* slipped out of her mouth. "Yeah, I'll go."

"Good. We could ride together if you wanted to pick me up. If you get too uncomfortable and want to go home, you'll have your own car."

"Then how are you going to get back home?" That's when Dana realized Taylor wouldn't be going home by herself. If not with her, Taylor would ride with someone else. "Ah. Never mind."

"That's poly, babe. It's okay if this world is not for you. It's not for everyone, and definitely not for those with weak souls."

Dana pushed away from the counter. "I'll see you Saturday."

"Nine. I'll be ready."

Just before nine o'clock, Dana arrived at Taylor's residence. Both her car and an oversized truck, outfitted with lifts and mud tires, sat in the driveway. Her chest pounded like a drum solo, which made her queasy. She knew she had to just get through the night. This first night, or their first proper date, in order to quell the anxiety building up inside of her ever since they met.

To her surprise, a man opened the door when she expected Taylor to answer. She stumbled over her words as she attempted to ask, "Is this Taylor's place?"

The tall and very large man stood back and allowed her to enter. "You must be Dana. Taylor is not ready yet. Hi. I'm Mark."

He extended his hand to her, as if it were nothing unusual to meet another person who might sleep with his wife that night. Dana gave an authoritative shake. "Yes. It's a pleasure to meet you."

Mark gestured down the hallway. "You can find her in the second-to-last bedroom. You can get her moving along now."

Dana nodded as she made her way down the hall with deliberate steps. She peered inside from the door and saw Taylor in the bathroom. Dana gave a wave. "Hey. Hi."

"Hey, babe. Did you meet Mark?" she remarked as she applied makeup to her face at the same time.

From the ground up, Dana took Taylor's knee-high socks that were worn over the fishnet stockings. The black and white plaid skirt only tangentially covered her tush, and the white dress shirt knotted closed at her waist. Taylor parted her hair in the middle and she wore pigtails on each side. After applying a fresh coat of lipstick, Taylor tossed the tube in the sink and strolled over to her.

Dana stated as she licked her lips, "You look fantastic."

Taylor drew her shirt just a hair's breadth away from her chest as she stood inches from Dana. "And I won't be wearing a bra."

When Dana looked at the cleavage, her breath caught in her throat and her eyes widened in surprise. Her mind rushed back and never had another woman teased her by going braless. She quickly dismissed the lustful thought, along with the memories of her past. Again, not being one to mention her true feelings, Dana let the moment slip away as she said, "Are you set to go?"

"You are so fucking adorable," Taylor said as she passed.

Dana stayed close behind Taylor as they made their way out of the bedroom. Unmade and obviously shared by two people, the king-size bed caught her eye. It meant Mark was more than just a roommate; they shared a life and a bed together. Taylor rummaged through her purse in the living room. After pulling her driver's license and credit card, she looked under her shirt with a complexed worry.

Dana used that move a couple of times, stuffing her cards in her bra, but Taylor appeared to be a little lost without hers. She made the offer, saying, "Do you want me to hold her stuff? I'll put it into my wallet."

"You're a doll." Taylor passed her cards to Dana.

Dana took her wallet out of the back pocket of her jeans. On a night when she did not wish to carry a purse or bag, Dana stole the classic male move of placing a wallet next to her ass. Taylor walked up to Mark, kissed him, and said, "I'll be out late. Don't wait up."

As they exited the front door, Mark shouted, "Have a good time, honey!"

"And he knows you're going to a sex club?" Dana questioned as they hustled toward the car.

Dana opened the car door for Taylor. Taylor remarked, "Yes. Everything is very ethical. He does not ask what I do, but I would never lie to him. Or you. In terms of my life and relationships, I'm an open book. Just ask if you want to know anything."

They arrived at the club, and as promised, Taylor paid for Dana's admission. The two women entered the dimly lit corridor, which led to a large room with bar tables in the center and booths along the perimeter. A dance floor with a floor-to-ceiling metal pole occupied one side of the room. When they arrived, there was not a large crowd, so it was easy to find a table where they could sit, converse, and people-watch. Taylor directed Dana to the back corner, where the only other couple sat against the wall.

The club did not serve alcoholic beverages, but they offered complimentary water to guests. Taylor strolled to the bar and procured bottles for them while

Dana remained at the table. When Taylor returned, she sat next to Dana on the padded bench, in front of which was a small café table. Taylor snuggled up to Dana as she lifted her arm. A clear indication they were a couple.

Guests continued to arrive. The club catered to straight couples, as Dana saw no other lesbian pairings. Even as they mingled, all couples were with the opposite sex. Dana didn't mind being the only lesbian in the club; she was at ease with her sexuality.

While Dana and Taylor cuddled and took in the atmosphere, people gradually filled in the empty spaces. From time to time, Taylor caressed Dana's face with her hand and kissed her. While Dana's muscles shook slightly from her heightened nerves, she found that staying still helped her unwind.

She heard a deep, husky groan from behind her as she surveyed the club from a full 360-degree vantage point. The instinct to turn her head toward the noise caused her to look behind her at a couple. Dana's eyes darted away when her gaze caught sight of something she cared not see. She leaned into Taylor and whispered, "The guy behind us is getting a blow job."

Taylor, insolent in her actions, peered behind Dana to see exactly that. She stood up, grabbed Dana's hand, and exclaimed, "Let's go exploring, babe!"

They walked hand in hand past the tables in the main common area and into a hallway. Down the hall, they entered a second large room with sofas, chairs, and a mattress in the center. Each of the alcoves along the wall contained a bed. There were doors for privacy but no of which were closed except for one. The room's farthest corner gave home to a large wooden X with a woman whose body contorted to resemble the shape. Behind her, a man used a paddle to slap her blazing red ass.

On the mattress in the center of the room, a black-clad man massaged the back of a naked woman while straddling her. Another man rubbed his own meat and next to him, a muscular blond gentleman stood buck naked and pounded himself into an exotic brunette.

In all of Dana's years, she had never, ever witnessed anything even remotely close to this club. She didn't know where to direct her attention. Everywhere her gaze wandered, she found herself confronted with some form of sexual interaction. In contrast, none of it fazed Taylor. She slid in between a few people leaning against the wall, spying like voyeurs. Dana scooted in next to her while her entire body shook inexplicably, though she had no fear. A tingling sensation in the center of her body strangely aroused her as she watched the surreal experiences around her.

Without a second thought, Dana grabbed Taylor by the hand and dragged her into a tiny bedroom behind them. She shut the door to get some privacy, then took Taylor's face in her hands and pulled them closer together. They kissed each other passionately, allowing the romance to exist between them rather than lust. Her fingers explored Taylor's flesh as she worked the buttons of Dana's top. Dana became more enamored with Taylor as she massaged the tender nipples under the white blouse. She lowered her mouth to Taylor's bountiful breasts. The moment her tongue touched the bud, it stiffened to attention.

Dana climbed Taylor's neck and returned to her mouth with a passionate kiss. Taylor's hands rested so gently on Dana's waist while Dana groped every piece of skin she touched. With a brief need for air, Dana stared straight at Taylor and said, "I so want to be with you."

Instead of giving Dana the green light, Taylor replied in the sweetest voice Dana had ever heard, "Will you be mad if I wanted to wait?"

Dana was not angry with Taylor for clam jamming her in the middle of a sex club. More than anything, shocked rocked her core. "No. Of course not."

Taylor grabbed Dana's cheeks and gave her another passionate kiss while taking a deep breath, drawing it into her chest. And once more, she reiterated her earlier statement. "Slow burn."

She could only relate it to a literary trope in which the two main characters don't actually become romantically involved until the very end of the story. If Taylor intended the same, it could be quite some time before they hooked up. Dana wanted more than just sex from their relationship, yet she secretly hoped things moved quickly thanks to Taylor's open door policy between her legs. Throughout their conversations, Taylor made it abundantly clear her sexuality was central to her being, and even bragged about her many escapades.

Dana helped Taylor button her shirt, then opened the door. With their hands clasped together, she followed Taylor out the door to a couch across the room, where they conversed with the massage therapist while others fucked around them.

An additional hour passed. Dana sat next to Taylor, while Taylor mingled with various guests around them. With free love all around her, Dana no longer averted her gaze from the events taking place directly in front of her. Taylor asked Dana if she wished to leave as soon as the masseuse departed. Dana shook her head, indifferent to the situation.

"Why don't we take off then?" Taylor stated.

"You want me to drive you home?"

"Yeah. I'm drained. It's been a long day."

Not how Dana planned the night would go, but she helped Taylor off the couch, and they left the club as a couple. On the way home, Taylor discussed the club, what she thought of it, and how it compared to others she visited in Colorado and Texas. She mentioned them visiting Flourdelis North again and even purchasing an annual membership to save money. In all of that, Taylor referred to the club as a place where they could be free to experiment together. Dana may have preferred sex in the comfort of her clean home; the idea of a special hangout excited her.

They arrived at Taylor's residence. She turned to Dana and said, "I really had a delightful time with you. I hope it opened your eyes to the polyamorous and swinger lifestyle I lead."

Dana grinned widely as it embarrassed her to say, "I really liked it. I mean, I never knew this kind of place existed, but I kind of want to go back."

She leaned across the seat and met Dana in the middle. They kissed. As they separated, Taylor remarked, "Good. We can have a safe place where we can be ourselves without the constraints of everyday life."

"Are you working tomorrow?"

"No. Luckily. Mark works, so I'll be home, recovering from this late-night outing."

"Why don't I come over and we spend the day together? Regardless of what we do. At least we'd be together."

"I'd love that. Mark leaves at six o'clock, so why not nine? If you're running late, message me."

"Perfect."

Taylor opened the car door after another quick kiss and exited before Dana could open her door and walk her to the house. Taylor smiled and waved as she approached the front door. That concluded their night. Dana drove contentedly home, ecstatic at the prospect of spending the day with this wonderful woman, who thrilled her to no end.

J ust before nine in the morning, Dana set out for Taylor's residence. She got a cup of coffee for herself and also bought one for Taylor at the same time. After such a late night and a somewhat early morning, it was the least she could do for her. It was Taylor's idea who proposed Dana's early arrival. Most likely, with Mark's work obligations, Taylor needed to rise with him.

Butterflies swarmed Dana's stomach on the drive to Taylor's house. With such high expectations for her day, she hardly slept the night before. When she finally dozed off, Dana dreamed about them being together. Dana's dream featured Mark and her pleasing Taylor at the same time. It wasn't exactly romantic, but she woke up to wet undies, so she didn't scoff at the possibility of living out that dream. So long as Mark understood Dana was off limits. She had absolutely no interest in having anyone of the male persuasion come anywhere near her body.

Taylor's vehicle sat in the drive, with the truck nowhere in sight. It relieved Dana to learn Mark's man parts wouldn't be near her or Taylor that day as Dana pulled up to the house. She strolled up the drive, drinks in hand, to the front door. She rapped on the white wooden door twice. Inside the house, the dog sniffed and barked at the door's threshold. When Taylor did not answer the door, Dana knocked once more.

Dana hummed to herself as the dog barked again at the door. Perplexed, Dana checked her watch. "Hmm. This is odd."

She waited a moment before knocking again, thinking Taylor must be in the shower. That time it was a little louder. It was strange for Taylor not to mention it in a text or call if the plans changed, even at the last minute. Dana grew concerned something might have happened. Maybe Taylor slipped inside. Or perhaps Taylor dozed off from being out extra later. After giving the door a few more knocks, Dana peered through the door's small round window in the middle of the door. She couldn't see much through the beveled glass, but she tried anyway. After one last knock went unanswered, Dana went back to her car.

She placed the coffees on the seat next to her, then retrieved her phone from her purse. Dana inspected her text messages, missed calls, and dating app for communications from Taylor. Not hearing from her, Dana sent Taylor a message instead. *Are you home?*

She waited for about two minutes before placing the key in the ignition. A reply arrived soon after. *I'm not home. I'm with Mark at the hospital. His BP dropped, and he passed out at work.*

The explanation for why Taylor hadn't answered the door made perfect sense. Dana felt bad for him and them. She responded. *I hope he feels better. I came by the house like we planned, but I understand. Please give him my best.*

Dana started the car, but she recognized it would be dangerous for her to text and drive at the same time. Taylor's message came through. ***Sorry. This is crazy shit. I'm so freaked out. I'm really sorry.***

Something seemed off as Taylor appeared to be a woman unprepared to deal with whatever medical issues had arisen. When Dana read the message, she realized even though Taylor had a very sexual personality, she never heard her use foul language. This led Dana to believe something may be seriously wrong. It wasn't important they spent time together that day. Her man came first. ***When you get home, you'll need to watch him closely. I'm gonna take off. We'll try this again another day. No worries. I understand. And again, I do hope he feels better.***

As Dana took one last look at the house, her stomach turned, and her heart sank. She had no intention of acting in a self-centered manner, but their timing never seemed to work out in their favor with their dates. Dana read Taylor's last message. *I know we had plans, but this was absolutely out of my hands today. I'm sorry.*

She put the car in drive and started driving back to her apartment. Instead of going back home, Dana took the day and treated herself to a massage and nails. She seldom pampered herself, but when the day started out disappointing, she needed a pick-me-up.

After a day at the spa, she stopped for lunch then hit her favorite department store, where she purchased several new pairs of jeans and a blazer for the upcoming winter. As she stepped out, the jewelry store next door caught her eye. She wandered around, eying the cases. Dana pulled out her wallet after being enticed by the bracelet and bought it with Taylor in mind. She'd give it to her on their next date whenever that would be.

After a day out, she returned home, threw her clothes in the washing machine, then flopped onto the sofa. Dana checked her phone to see if Taylor sent her a text message. She wasn't expecting a deluge of messages, but she hoped for a brief update on Mark's health. Dana did not send a message because she did not wish to bother Taylor, especially if Mark's condition worsened.

She expected to receive a message the following morning, but her inbox was empty. Not receiving any messages from Taylor was unusual. One or two messages from her always waited for her when she woke up. There might have been a poem she read and wished to share, or a link to something Dana ought to view. Since they began exchanging text messages, it had become a standard practice to wake up to a few messages.

On that Monday morning, while she sipped her coffee, Dana browsed the social networking site they both used. Dana attempted to tag Taylor in an aptly-timed inspirational quote. Her eyebrows arched in interest as Taylor's name did not come up in her search. Dana tapped the screen and navigated to the messenger program, where she viewed their previous conversation, but it lacked the option to send a message at the bottom of the screen.

"What the—," Dana said, stopping mid-sentence her stomach churned. Mr. Jinx meowed while rubbing himself against her leg. She kneeled down to pet him and said, "I know. I'm just as confused as you are."

Dana changed social media platforms and conducted searches on the other two she knew Taylor used. She could no longer view Taylor's accounts for either of them. Dana said to no one but herself, "Okay. What the hell happened to Taylor?"

It was inexplicable how everything disappeared in a matter of hours. A knot formed in her stomach, and a sneaking suspicion caused her hands to tremble. On each social media platform, Dana conducted a search for Taylor using her company's credentials. Taylor's profile appeared on each. At that moment, Dana realized. "Taylor blocked me?"

Dana set her phone down and, with her head in her hands and the rewind button activated in her mind, she attempted to figure out what the hell had gone wrong. The only thing she could think of was the club and pulling her into the room, but even if it was her forwardness that turned Taylor off, Dana stopped immediately when Taylor did not want to take things further. In other words, Dana was the epitome of gentlemanhood. *So, what the hell happened?*

# SCOTT

Dana disappeared from her friends' lives over the following week. With random bouts of tears, the last thing she needed was to explain how attached she became to a woman she didn't know well enough. So, she ignored them. No calls. No messages. She could not fathom where her relationship with Taylor turned sour. It had been almost perfect. Taylor had a beautiful spirit and always saw the best in others. She never made a negative remark about anyone, and her optimistic outlook on life always made Dana feel better.

When they made plans and something unexpected came up, they both expressed regret at having to cancel. It wasn't like Dana had a negative attitude about it. In the messages to Taylor, she wished Mark well and did not complain once about another canceled plan. Dana read the messages multiple times in an effort to find some explanation behind Taylor's sudden decision to block her across the board on every social media platform.

She'd shared her soul with this woman and embraced a lifestyle with which Dana may not have agreed, but she expressed it to Taylor. However, the woman who occupied her every waking moment cast her aside and erected a barrier that prevented Dana from even asking why. Dana considered storming over to Taylor's house and confronting her, but decided against it. What did Dana do to get herself blocked?

The situation perplexed her so much and absorbed so much of her attention that she didn't hear the front door to her shop open. Scott's voice emanating from the design room jolted her out of her trance. "Are you too good to answer the phone anymore?"

"I'm sorry, Scott. Something's got me a little preoccupied and I'm not in the right headspace," Dana responded as she spun in her office chair.

"Something or someone? Either way, you don't look good. What's the matter, honey?" Scott asked.

Scott always knew when Dana had problems or drama she didn't want to talk about. When it came to interpreting his friend's moods, he excelled at it. It wasn't worth keeping secret, so Dana spent the next thirty minutes providing Scott with a play-by-play account of her relationship with Taylor, hoping he or she could pinpoint the exact moment when the shit hit the proverbial fan.

When Dana finished, Scott said, "It sounds like the woman is bat shit crazy. Good riddance."

"Scott, that does not help. I'm heartbroken because she made me believe our relationship had lasting potential. She may not have been a lifer, but I could see her lasting for a good year or two. What the fuck?"

"This excessive use of the word 'fuck' is so not you. She did a real number on you. This isn't a good thing. Michelle? I can understand why she would use such language, but you? This girl has changed you into someone I do not recognize. Wifey did not even inspire this level of hatred in your normal angsty self."

There was no disputing Scott's wisdom in the matter. Dana was not the type of person to use a lot of foul language, not even during the trying times of the divorce. Maybe shit or damn every once in a while, but Taylor brought out this very pissed off woman, and Dana didn't like her at all. "What's my problem?"

"The problem isn't with you."

"Then why is it I can't seem to find anyone who isn't off her rocker? I liked this one a lot." Dana hated the whine in her voice, but it was hard to control as she hit rock bottom. The corner of her eye glistened with a single tear. She wiped it before it could fall.

"I'd like to see this woman. What is her screen name?" Scott questioned.

Compared to the photo-heavy social media platforms, Scott preferred one where users could upload videos. After Dana walked him through the steps of finding her, he looked her up on his phone. "She published a post on Wednesday. When did you say that all of this took place?"

"Sunday. Monday."

Scott mentioned the video and increased the volume as Dana peered over his shoulder.

Taylor's angelic voice spoke over the speaker, saying, "Present circumstances have me feeling persistent sadness twenty-four seven. There just doesn't seem to be any good people in the world who understand what I need, so I fear this may be the end of my poly life. Just when I think I've found a woman who understands me, she turns on me with crazy eyes and starts banging on my door and staring through my windows."

During Taylor's video, Dana interjected, "I didn't bang on her door."

"I wouldn't think you would," Scott added.

Taylor then asked the camera, "Where are my normal people? When do I finally get to sit back, relax, and hang out with my two favorite people? There are no women I can find who are even worth it. I have a lot to offer. Though I've lived a happy polyam life for the past twelve years, I fear the end is near when even the most basic of my needs aren't being met. It's so discouraging!"

The video cut out. Dana had no words to say. She wanted to scream and yell at the screen, but she knew that wouldn't accomplish anything. If anything, it proved Taylor right. Crazy. Not normal.

Scott remained silent as Dana contemplated the video. She rose from her office chair and walked into the design room with her eyes directed upwards. In the end, she confronted Scott with the question, "Do you really think she believes I'm some crazy, obsessed person? If she feels threatened by me, can she report it to the police? What if she puts some kind of restraining order against me?"

He pursued her, took both of her hands, and spoke soothing words to her. "One, you did nothing wrong. Two, getting a restraining order is a lot of work. You'd have to be threatening her, and she has no evidence to suggest you did."

"I didn't!"

"I know. It is therefore nonexistent. She's just talking out of her own ass. The woman has some serious mental issues. Let her go, and move on with your life. You are better off without her. Find someone who wants you, not a harem of sex slaves."

"Scott, I've given it my all, and I'm sick and tired of the fact that other people don't think I'm good enough. I've lowered my standards, raised them, but nothing I do brings me closer to finding happiness. My only other choice is to grovel my way back to Bridgette and give her permission to live a poly life as well. If I accepted it from Taylor, then why not from Bridgette? If nothing else, Bridgette loved me."

"You'd feel just as lonely as if you were by yourself."

"Exactly. What's the difference between the two? I'm over it." Dana pulled her phone out of her pocket and uninstalled every single dating app on it. She accepted she would be single and was at peace with it. Relationships created unnecessary drama and anxiety in her life.

Scott questioned. "Fine. So, what are you going to do now? "

"Get drunk!" Dana said as she grabbed her bag. "Come on, we're going out." Even though it was still an hour before closing time, Dana switched the open sign to closed as they exited the store. At that point, Dana didn't give a damn about anything. If a woman wanted to call her crazy, she would act crazy, such as closing the store earlier than usual.

They met at the bar and ordered a round of tequila shots right away. Instead of grabbing a booth as usual, Dana sat on a bar stool so she could admire the bartender. The married and very straight bartender placed the shot glasses in front of Dana and Scott and poured the liquor.

Dana beckoned to the woman with a wave of her hand. "You too. I'm going to buy you a shot as well."

The bartender put another glass on the counter, then poured. They all downed the shot of tequila in one swift motion at the same time. Dana said, "Again!"

She poured another round of drinks for Dana and Scott, but she said, "One's my limit. Thanks."

Dana had a thirst for beer like a seaman, but she couldn't handle hard liquor. It traveled straight to her blood. She ordered a third and gulped it down.

Scott excused himself for a restroom break. Dana, lonely without him to talk to, addressed the bartender and said, "Apparently, I'm a crazy woman who can't find love. I don't know whether it's been twenty or fifty dates, but not even one of them wants me. One of them did, but the crazed woman made a sound like a sasquatch when I ate her out. Nope. I'm crazy. In fact, she went as far as to call me crazy. Or not normal. I'm normal, aren't I?"

The bartender poured another, but also sat a glass of water in front of Dana, and asked, "Are you drinking for fun or are you aiming for a pitiful drunken stupor this evening? "

"Why are you not gay?" Dana asked.

The woman laughed. "I like 'em hard."

"I've been coming here for years, and I still don't know your name."

"Jess."

Dana extended her hand to Jess. "I'm Dana. It's a pleasure to meet you and not sleep with you. How about another shot?"

"Same here." Jess brought out a bowl of nuts from behind the counter and set them on the table, saying, "And I'm cutting you off for a bit. Eat, then we'll talk about more shots."

Scott returned to the bar and took a seat next to her. As he slid onto the stool, Dana said to him, "Even Jess is cutting me out of her life, and we haven't even had sex yet."

"Jess is straight, babe. You'll never get near her snatch," Scott joked as he grabbed a handful of nuts and tossed them in his mouth.

"Perhaps I should be more like you. Every night, find a hottie, pour some alcohol in them, and go to town. You seem happy. I can be gay and happy like you."

He rolled his eyes even though Dana wasn't paying him much attention as she scanned the room, looking for any pretty women who might find her attractive. Scott stated, "I'd be pissed at you right now if she hadn't just dumped you. I'm going to let that slide since I know it's the tequila talking."

Dana snapped her attention back to him as soon

as she heard the upset tone. She drew closer to him and took his arm in her grasp as she leaned in. "I'm a horrible person. This is why Taylor dumped me and blocked me. I'm just a disgusting—"

"Stop! We do lower ourselves to fit someone else's idea of who we are, even after a few Tequila shots. Don't forget it, baby, we're queens."

"I'm a lesbian, Scott. I'm a king. You're the queen," Dana continued on and on, saying whatever came to her mind, most of which made no sense to her or anyone else. That was, until Scott's eyes fell upon a hottie at the back of the bar. Dana was not too drunk to notice. She pushed him off the stool. "Go get 'em, tiger."

Scott sat back down. "No. It's all about you tonight."

"I don't need you to watch over me like a baby." She pointed at Jess and said, "I'm going to have another round, then go home by myself like I always do. I ate the nuts, so pour me a couple more."

Jess sauntered over to Dana, giving Scott a way out. "I got her. Have a fun time. She'll be fine."

He jumped off the stool as Jess pulled a bottle out from under the counter. She leaned on the counter instead of pouring the shot. Dana's eyes drew to Jess's breasts, which filled out the tank top she wore. She slowly brought them upward to Jess's eyes, who said, "If I pour the shots, you'll have to take an Uber home or I'll send a police officer to take you home. Or I can give you another glass of water, and in an hour or two you can drive yourself home. Which sounds better?"

"Is the cop hot?" Dana smirked.

"Very," Jess said with a smile, then looked toward the door to see a woman sitting at the far end of the counter.

Dana looked in the same direction as Jess and saw a beautiful Latina woman sitting on the last stool. She squinted in the light because the woman looked familiar, but she couldn't place her. She thought about all the bad dates she'd been on in the past year, but she couldn't remember any with a Hispanic woman. A wave of emotion swept through her, leaving her eyes brimming with tears. Dana gave in. "Water."

Jess tucked the bottle of Tequila beneath the counter and reached for a bottle of water instead. With a huff, Dana grabbed it and slid off the stool. She crossed the floor and hid herself in a booth at the back of the bar. Dana knew it was not safe for her to drive yet. The alcohol hadn't messed up her sense of right and wrong, just her ability to focus her eyes. She needed a place where she could cry in peace.

From where she sat, she took in the entire bar. The woman, who looked familiar, slipped off her stool, walked to the back, and stopped in front of Scott. They talked for a moment. Occasionally, one of them glanced over at her. The dreadful and agonizing realization she was the subject of conversation struck her. She tucked herself in and drank her water, so she arrived home in one piece.

Dana went to the bar to pay her tab when the room stopped spinning enough for her to walk. Jess waved her off. "Your friends have covered it."

Her ears perked up at the plural, but she thought Jess had made a mistake and meant Scott paid for her drinks. Dana took twenty dollars out of her purse and put it in the tip glass. "Thanks."

She crossed the bar with deliberate steps and pushed through the front door. As she made her way to her vehicle, she became cognizant of another person behind her. Dana glimpsed someone, but she didn't stop long enough to see who it was. She hurried her steps, and as soon as she reached her vehicle, she spun around, brandishing her car key like a knife.

Dana lowered it when she saw the familiar woman from the bar, whose dark hair flowed over her shoulders. The woman said, "I'm just making sure you get to your car all right. Are you okay with driving?"

Dana drew a sarcastic tone from the depths of her chest. "I'm fine. Want to see me walk a fucking straight line?"

The woman gave a casual shrug. "I watched you walk; I know you are sober enough. It's the upset part. Care to talk?"

"I don't even know who the fuck you are, so no. I don't want to talk to a stranger about my fucked-up life." Dana opened her car door and shut herself inside.

The woman took a step toward the car, but Dana cranked the engine and backed out of the parking spot in a hurry. As the car moved, the light from the poles above hit the woman just right. The woman's face flashed into her memory. Officer Cynthia Morales.

*Shit!* Dana thought as she continued in reverse, not wanting to stop because she felt like a fool. Dana dropped her head and drove away, hoping she'd never see her again.

# CYNTHIA

Taylor hadn't communicated with Dana in nearly a month. Although she acknowledged to her closest friends and herself that she was done with Taylor, she continued to check her social media accounts to see if she had posted anything new. The need for assurance that Taylor had stopped spreading untrue rumors about her was more of a need than an obsession. Dana checked to make sure there was nothing new, then she logged off. After a month of nothing, Dana came to the firm conclusion that Taylor had moved on and was no longer interested in her.

The product from Atlanta arrived, which took a significant amount of her time. She put everything she had purchased for Mother's Day, Valentine's Day, and the spring holidays in storage. On the other hand, the Christmas items remained in stock. She made holiday arrangements in the containers, photographed them, and posted them on her website. Dana prepared for her annual open house, which always took place the weekend following Halloween, by hanging holiday decorations in her shop. For that weekend, she typically enlisted Scott and Michelle's assistance because she was well known for drawing large crowds to see her inventive decorating ideas.

It was the last box to be emptied before all Atlanta market-ordered goods became available for purchase. The store appeared to be prepared for the holiday season. Dana placed the shelves with the dried lavender plants. The front door swung open behind her. When she looked over her shoulder, she noticed a pair of black work pants and heavy black shoes. As her gaze moved upward, she observed the utility belt, which held a gun and a taser. The button-down shirt clung to a bulletproof vest emblazoned with Morales' name.

Up until Cynthia stood in front of her, Dana had completely forgotten about the night she got drunk. Despite her best efforts, the smirk on her face was actually embarrassment. She would claim she had no memory of the incident if Cynthia brought it up.

She got up and dusted her pants off before approaching the counter. "Hello, Cynthia. What can I do for you today? Want to buy Mom some more flowers?"

"No. No flowers, but I might have to look at those trees you just set out. My cousin loves lavender," Officer Morales said as she followed Dana to the counter.

Dana moved behind it, grabbing her order pad and preparing to assist the officer with whatever she needed. "Well, those make excellent Christmas presents. Together with poinsettias and amaryllis, they would make the ideal holiday garden."

A small chuckle escaped Cynthia's lips as she moved forward. "You're a good salesperson because I now want to buy one for each of my cousins, but I would go bankrupt because I have so many."

"Well, you know I give the police discount, but we haven't discussed prices, so you don't know if it would break you."

"Touché. That we haven't," Officer Morales said, pulling her phone from her pocket. "But I'm actually not here for shopping today, more like official business."

Dana cocked her head and her eyes widened. Her mind raced as she tried to recall something she had done wrong. She turned quickly to Taylor, wondering if she had filed a formal complaint against her. Perhaps a piece of software informed Taylor that she had visited her page. "What kind of business?"

After a few taps, Officer Morales displayed the phone's screen to Dana and stated, "I'm looking for this woman."

Dana couldn't stop laughing when she saw her online dating profile on Cynthia's screen. Using a dating site wasn't illegal, but it wasn't a particularly proud moment for her either. Following the unfortunate events involving Taylor, she uninstalled the app from her phone but kept her account intact. "Yes. That would be me."

"I'm actually here to do a wellness check because I swiped right on this profile and messaged her, but she didn't respond. She hadn't even been online since the beginning of the month, so I started to worry," Cynthia said as she tucked her phone back into her pocket.

She quickly covered her mouth to conceal her grin as her cheeks became flushed. Dana pressed her lips together, amused by Cynthia's use of her power to call her out on the profile. Ignoring most of Cynthia's initial statement, Dana responded, "That is correct. I haven't logged on. In fact, I deleted it."

"I'm not sure if I should be worried."

"Why should that worry you?"

"Most people delete these types of apps once they find what they're looking for."

"Hardly. It's more like it doesn't exist at all."

Cynthia placed her hand on her chest to shield her emotions. "Ouch. I'd hate to think I didn't exist."

Dana laughed. "I've been on over a dozen terrible dates that were so painful and terrifying that I'm not sure how sane people find each other."

"Nonetheless, here we are. We found each other," Cynthia explained. She took out her phone again and handed it to Dana after a few taps and swipes. "This is my profile. Tell me if you'd dismiss me or swipe for more information."

She shook her head emphatically to show her disapproval. Dana backed up and held up her hands as Cynthia shoved the phone in her direction. Finally, Cynthia set it down on the counter and waited. Naturally, Dana looked at the phone, where she saw a Latina woman with long dark hair and the most incredible chocolate-colored eyes. That drunken night flashed before her mind again. The bar patron who tagged along with her to the car. The person she had threatened to stab with her car key.

Dana slowly took the phone in her hands and read the profile.

*Latina blood with a big heart for friends and family. Hookups are not cool. Instead of a revolving door, I want a long-term relationship with a kind, cultured, and intelligent person. Must care about family, because I have a large one that is the most valuable thing I own.*

Dana slid the phone back onto the counter and pursed her lips. Both stared at each other for a while before Dana finally broke the silence. "I would have probably swiped for your information and asked you out. Then you would have arrived wearing your uniform and, while we were finishing our meal, you would have dashed off after some bad guy, guns blazing, and I would have never seen you again."

And then Cynthia pressed, "So the job is making you not want to say yes?"

"Technically, it's the fact that I've never been asked out, even though I know how it'll end, which is that I'll never see you again."

She gave a slight nod before picking up the phone and removing it from the counter. Cynthia turned away and walked out the door, her phone back in her pocket. Dana felt terrible as she watched Cynthia leave, but after everything she had been through over the course of the previous year, the last thing she wanted to do was watch another failed date or relationship, especially so close to the holidays. Just being alone was terrible, but she didn't need a broken heart on top of that.

The holiday open house party at Mod Botanicals was a smashing success. Dana took a short break in the back of the store as the crowds thinned out so she could relax. It was imperative for her to take a break, even if it was just for five minutes, because she still had a lot of cleaning to do. The sole objective of those few moments was to provide a brief break for her feet for a momentary reprieve. With the contracts she had booked for holiday sales and decorating, her mind was racing. A lot of her clients loved the new trend of using lots of wood and other natural materials. She even signed a contract with a luxury hotel, which would have to be taken into account.

After taking a deep breath, she cupped her hands over her eyes. As soon as Michelle poked her head into the office, her break was over. "There's a lady out front who wants to order a bunch of holiday gardens. Whatever the hell that is. She mentioned using the lavender trees?"

"Wow," Dana exclaimed as she slowly exhaled and stood up. "I'll be there in a second."

Michelle grinned. "She's also pretty hot. I'd fix your hair."

"Shut up. I already told you. I've had enough of this

crazy ass dating nonsense, no matter how attractive the other person is."

When Dana turned the corner and re-entered the showroom, she paused momentarily when she saw Cynthia at the counter. And when Michelle said the woman was hot, she wasn't kidding. Her face reddened at Cynthia's sly glance, and she immediately wished she had followed Michelle's advice and fixed her hair. Dana didn't hesitate for more than a brief instant before approaching the officer and saying, "Officer Morales. I see that you've decided to take me up on the offer of the plant baskets for your... cousins? Right?"

At the mention of her formal name, Cynthia's eyes became less bright and her smile faded a little. Dana accomplished her goal, which was to drive a wedge between business and pleasure. There would be no pleasure between them.

Cynthia responded with a yes as soon as she saw Dana making her way behind the counter. "I'd like to buy some for a few of my cousins."

She reached her hand under the counter and pulled out a notepad. Dana pushed it towards her with a pen and said, "If you could jot down their names and addresses, I'll write up their orders in the morning. I have all your information saved in my system, and I can send the receipts to your email address. When do you need them sent over?"

After clearing her throat, Cynthia turned her attention back to Dana after a quick glance at Michelle and Scott, who were still hiding in the design room.

"Sometime before Christmas. Whenever is easiest for you."

"Great. And, as I mentioned, I'll include the discount for our law enforcement." Dana sported a fake grin.

Cynthia proceeded to write the addresses down on the notepad, and when she was finished, she placed the pen on top of the notepad and slid it across the counter. "Perfect. Thank you."

The police officer sulked out of the room afterward. Dana saw her leave and breathed a sigh of relief as the door closed behind her. Michelle and Scott sprinted out of the room, and Michelle yelled, "What the hell was that?"

"What?" Dana questioned.

Michelle remarked, "You were literally a total bitch to her."

"No, I wasn't. I was polite and businesslike."

"And a jackass to a woman who wanted to ask you out," Michelle confirmed.

Dana shouted to her friends, "I'm not dating! Let it fucking go!"

Scott responded, "Not everyone is like Taylor."

"No, they're not. They're like Tiffany, Britt, and Angie. Seriously, I can't handle it when others laugh at me, insult me, or even growl at me when I like them. I've spent more time recovering from the trauma caused by these women than I have having fun. It won't happen again. I'm done."

"Then what? You're going to spend the rest of your life single?" Michelle asked, equally as frustrated as

Dana was with herself.

"What exactly is wrong with that?"

"Because all you do is sulk, and you're not very pleasant to be around. If you want to be single, get your head out of your ass and bring Dana out into the open," Michelle explained. Instead of allowing Dana to continue arguing, she grabbed her bag and jacket and left the store.

Dana remained silent. She turned, her heart racing with annoyance and her eyes glinting with sadness. Scott pressed his lips together and nodded, "She's right. We love you, but we don't like the person you've become."

When Scott walked out, she opened her mouth, ready to defend herself. Alone in the store, she hurriedly locked the entrance. She noticed her friends leaning against their automobiles as she peered out the wall of windows that overlooked the parking lot. Dana's eyes welled up with tears as she grabbed for the rope to turn off the open sign. Just outside the store, she noticed Cynthia sitting on the hood of her car.

After a brief exchange of looks, Dana turned off the lights in the storefront, which left the showroom in complete darkness. Dana retreated to the back of the room as soon as Cynthia stood up, showing her displeasure with the situation.

Things just weren't working out. She dabbed at her wet cheeks to wipe the tears. Passing the front desk, she quickly grabbed Cynthia's paperwork along with the other work tickets and proceeded to her office. Instead of leaving and heading home, she went back to her desk and entered a number of orders so that she would have less work to do on the following Monday.

When she got to Cynthia's orders, she pulled up her billing details. She quickly took a look at her mailing address. The two people shared the same postal code. Dana looked at the maps and checked out the ranch house with the big front yard. She huffed in exasperation at her own curiosity and resumed entering the orders. Dana scanned the paper, entering each address, until she reached the bottom of the page, where Cynthia had left a comment.

*And yet, you are seeing me again. And here is me asking you out... I'd like to take you out because you haven't smiled in a while. Smiling suits you.*

Michelle confronted her on the matter. Scott also knew it. A woman she scarcely knew had even noticed the melancholy on her face. She dreaded going out. When it came to Orlando's dating scene, it felt like a trip to the hell and back. Even if she changed her mind and decided to date Cynthia, the fact that she treated her like a piece of trash damaged her chances.

Dana pushed the papers aside and turned off her computer because she no longer cared about her work. She'd get everything done in the morning. After gathering her personal belongings, Dana shut down the rest of the store and left through the front door.

To her surprise, Cynthia continued to lean against the vehicle. The gradual upward movement of Dana's lips finally brought a smile to her face, although it was not one of joy and happiness. It was a painful realization that her friends were all correct. She had been miserable for so long that she had forgotten how to feel anything else besides depression.

Instead of approaching her automobile, she approached Cynthia, who sat on the hood of her vehicle. "Bored tonight with nothing to do?"

"More like optimistic and probably delusional," Cynthia answered, still seated atop the car with her hands on the steel hood.

Dana never took her eyes off of Cynthia. "It is the delusional part that concerns me."

"I've heard. When they've had a few drinks, your pals become pretty talkative. I can see why they're your friends." Cynthia's laughter lessened the tension slightly.

"Birds of a feather. Sorry about what happened that night. That was not my finest hour."

"Everyone has them. Forgotten."

Dana cocked her head, forming a downward arch with her brow. "And when did you have drinks with my friends?"

"A couple of weeks back. They came in one night without you, and I bought them a round so I could investigate." Cynthia shrugged and slid off the hood before leaning against it.

"The cop always on duty?"

"Off duty, like right now. I had finally worked up the courage to ask you out, but as you drank more tequila than a quinceañera, I began to wonder what the hell had happened to you and began to second-guess my decision."

"Again, not my finest moment."

"I've seen my fair share of lawn vomit and walks of shame, believe me. Despite your current moodiness, your pals created a really beautiful picture of you that I'd like to get to know."

"You want to go out with me even though that I was a complete bitch to you and them?"

Cynthia took a step closer, smug and confident. She narrowed the distance between them and nodded while pressing her lips into a line. She didn't speak a word, but the fire in her eyes communicated everything Dana needed to know.

Dana's mind wandered solely to the numerous dates she had been on, each of whom had their own disturbing take on reality. Dana replied, "Are you crazy?"

She didn't back down. "Probably."

"Anyone who would consider dating me is insane."

"Most likely." Cynthia stood solidly on both feet.

"Do you growl during sex?" Dana asked with an unflinching gaze in her direction.

Cynthia lowered her head and suppressed a chuckle as she shook her head cryptically. "Although I had hoped for dinner first, do you want me to growl?"

Her hand rose to Cynthia's chest and pressed into her. After shaking her head, Dana gazed upward. "No. I'm worried I'm going to fall for you and end up regretting it when it all turns to shit."

"Why don't we have dinner first?"

"Because that is where it all begins. Dinner. Chaos. Crazy."

Cynthia grabbed Dana's hand, which was still resting on her chest. She clutched it in her hands. Their eyes searched each other for a sign of hope. "Then let's skip dinner and start with dessert," she proposed.

"You want to sleep with me already?" Dana asked, worried that her sanity might be slipping away.

Cynthia laughed in the cool night air, "I was thinking more like pie. Just two blocks away, there's a diner that serves a mean apple pie."

Dana's cheeks turned bright crimson as she wished she could undo the past few statements she'd made. "Perhaps it's me, and I'm the crazy one in this."

"I'd only think you were crazy if you turned down this pie."

Dana agreed to meet Cynthia two blocks away at the diner. She'd never been there before, so she relied on Cynthia's recommendation.

They entered the diner together. The hostess immediately greeted them. "Morales. Look at yourself outside of your uniform. You clean up nicely!"

"Thank you, Mae. Is my usual table available?"

"Sure is," the hostess, Mae, replied as she smirked and welcomed them in.

Cynthia lightly squeezed Mae's arm as she passed. Dana read the vibe, or tried to, and recognized many of Bridgette's smug mannerisms when engaging in conversation with gorgeous girls. Mae may be lovely if her hair wasn't in a bun and she didn't appear like a maid from a 1970s sitcom. Cynthia seemed like the type who would let the woman take the lead, but since Dana didn't know which table was the "regular" one, she let Cynthia walk through the diner to the back corner. She motioned Dana to seat across from her at the table.

As Dana scooted in, she asked, "So, this is Cynthia Morales' throne?"

She laughed. "More like Chuy Morales. My father. He, too, was a cop. For forty years, he strolled up in the mornings for his cup of coffee and eggs. Every night after his work, he'd come here for a slice of pie before heading home. This was where he always sat, day and night. He enjoyed routine."

Dana realized that her last remark brimmed with arrogance. She was passing judgment on the woman's private table and the provocative winks only an insider would understand. The anecdote revealed a side of Cynthia consistent with her dating profile. Family was everything. "Did your father retire?"

"Passed away." Cynthia's eyes did not lose their natural brightness and contentment when she addressed it; it appeared as though she had made her peace with the fact that he had passed away. "And not to scare you away since I'm in the same line of work as him, but it was in the line of duty that he died."

Dana did not listen to Cynthia when she told her not to hold the new information against her. It marks another checkbox in the list of reasons not to date her. "I am sorry to hear that. You don't worry that it might happen to you?"

"I am but if you allow fear to dictate your emotions, you'll never live. Accidents involving motor vehicles are a leading cause of death worldwide; should I be apprehensive about getting behind the wheel? Because of my father, I decided to join the police force. He bled blue blood. It was an integral part of who he was, and he took great pride in embracing it. My brothers are all police officers, too."

Mae ambled down to the table with a glass of water, two mugs, and a pot of coffee. She set Cynthia's mug down and poured. She eyed Dana. "Would you want to have some coffee, honey?"

Dana wasn't the type of person who liked their

coffee piping hot right from the pot. She was more like a fancy sweetened with white mocha kind of person. Dana declined with a courteous grin, "The water is good. Thanks."

From across the booth, Cynthia asked, "Are you going to trust me with the apple pie?"

A hesitant grin crossed Dana's face once more. "Sure. If you claim it's killer. Let's do it."

"Two slices of Dad's favorite."

"Right away," Mae remarked as she took the solitary menu and left them alone.

The two women stared at one another; one was at ease in her usual booth, while the other was remained very aloof. Dana remained reserved because she expected the ball dropping and their unofficial date going entirely off the rails. Love was not on her side.

When Dana remained silent, Cynthia assumed control of the conversation. "Your friends spoke quite highly of you, and I'd like to get to know you, but there is this incredibly thick barrier between us. I could ask you question after question, but I don't believe it would allay your concerns about me or anyone else at this moment."

"You are correct. It wouldn't." Dana wrapped the wall around her so tightly that she nearly suffocated.

"That's okay because I'll tell you my life story while we eat pie. My father was a police officer, which you already know. Initially, I had no intention of following in his footsteps. Instead, I wanted to become a basketball star. There wasn't much of a demand for women's basketball because the sport wasn't nearly as popular as it is today. I was decent. Still am. On the court, I'll give my nephews a run for their money."

"I can sort of see that. I wasn't particularly good at sports," Dana interjected.

Cynthia pointed in her direction. "This is how I plan to get you to open up. See, I already know something about you. No sports."

She laughed and imitated the act of locking her mouth closed. "Continue on."

"Okay. Back then, my family held many traditional values, so being openly gay was not an option. I had a secret girlfriend, and we decided it would be easier if we lived together. I needed a job to do that. Attending college would not pay the rent. I joined the police force because my brothers had all joined and were making enough money for their wives and families."

"Did your parents object to you moving in with your girlfriend?"

"Actually, we never reached that point. After the academy and after I had a steady paycheck, she got pregnant because she wasn't actually gay."

Dana hid her laughter while shaking her head. "I had one of these as well. It's all fun and games until things get serious, at which point they no longer want to play house."

"Exactly. I didn't want to leave the force to return to college as planned, so I remained on the force. I met my first long-term girlfriend when I was injured on the job—and no, it wasn't a bullet wound. I slipped and cut my hand quite severely. She was the medic who cared for me."

"Is that not somewhat unethical?" Dana questioned, albeit in a lighthearted manner.

"True, but I was young at the time, and she was quite attractive in her nurse's uniform."

"Typical lesbian," Dana joked.

"I liked her for reasons other than her beauty." Cynthia called Dana on her snide nod and sneering grin. "You've never started a relationship because of someone's appearance?"

Again, Cynthia air-locked her mouth shut. "I'm not saying anything."

"Fine. We were together for exactly ten years. The relationship was rocky, which was partly my fault. I won't lie. In my youth, I was a very jealous person. Here I was a beat officer, while she was advancing in her medical career. I never felt good enough for her, and we decided it was best to end the relationship."

"I know couples who met when they were very young and are still together. Like, in high school. I have no idea how they did it. Thirty years or more together is an accomplishment."

Cynthia leaned into the table and asked directly. "I'll attempt to remove a layer here. What is your longest relationship number?"

The slices of pie were brought out, but neither of them took a bite at once. Dana hesitated before finally responding, "Twenty. Four of them were legally wed."

"Ouch." Cynthia said. "Mine was eleven. Angela. You know, the person I shouldn't have been jealous of, I was, and the person I should have questioned, I didn't."

They finally took a bite of the pie. Immediately after closing her mouth around the fork, Dana moaned into it. With her mouth full, Dana exclaimed, "Wow. This is amazing."

"I told you. You ought to have more confidence in me." Cynthia amusedly wiggled her eyebrows.

"I lost faith in women quite some time ago."

Cynthia shrugged. "I did too. I finally became lonely enough to resort to a dating app." She extended her hand in an attempt not to offend her. "No offense intended. I don't know why you posted a profile, but I assume it was for the same reason I did."

"No offense taken. Some people had good luck with them, but I was scraping the bottom of the barrel. I came to the conclusion that it was just me. I mean, how awful can an entire year of women be? I eventually looked for the common factor, and I discovered that it was me."

"And thus a little bit more of the wall drops down." After taking a slice of the pie, Cynthia dabbed her mouth. "And this is the reason you're so against dating?"

"Fuck," Dana muttered, lowering her head. When she looked up, she saw Cynthia's sexy dark eyes scrutinizing her. ""Do you know that when you came into my store spouting you had official business, I swear you were there to serve me papers because this woman I tried to date accused me of being some type of stalker."

Cynthia began to giggle across the table from her. She eventually laughed aloud. "I don't see that in you. Is that what made you eventually turn down all other women?"

"Yes!" She nailed the nail on the head with that, but Dana knew she had let down her guard with Cynthia. To reclaim her dignity, she tightened her shoulders even more. With her arms folded across her chest, Dana reclined back in her booth with her back straight. "I should go. Let me cover the pies."

"And the wall goes back up."

Dana gave a headshake. "It does, I apologize. Again, let me pay for the pie."

"Don't worry about it or the pies. Maybe we should give it another shot and aim for coffee one morning?"

"I don't want to date."

"It's not a date; it's coffee."

Dana didn't respond and instead slid out of the room after taking a ten dollar bill out of her purse and setting it on the table. "Cynthia, it's been a pleasure. Stay safe, and I'll send those holiday planters for you."

S weat dripped down her back as she climbed on top of Cynthia. In an upward arch, Dana raised her breasts. Her heart raced, and her breathing became labored. Dana reached her peak and opened her mouth to cry, but instead of ecstatic cries, the room filled with the annoying and shrill bray of a donkey.

Dana jumped out of bed and gasped in the shadows. She looked next to her, not to discover Cynthia, but to find Mr. Jinx snoring. She sank back onto the pillows, placing her hand against her chest to slow her gasps. She threw back the sheets and got out of bed because nothing could bring her back to a state of rest. The house stayed tidy while she lived alone. Even her interests were nonexistent, so she had nothing to do.

Depression sapped every ounce of strength necessary to consider going on a hike or early morning walk. Dana rummaged through the closet and retrieved a few of treasured photo albums. Her friends laughed at the idea of preserving solid and tangible items such as photographs, but in a society dominated by technology, Dana lacked faith that digital photographs would last forever.

Dana once possessed an aptitude for photography.

She owned a number of cameras and shot film in every location she and Bridgette visited. Dana always carried a pocket camera, even before she was in a relationship. When she moved in with Bridgette, she brought boxes full of prints with her. She enjoyed flipping through them, but Bridgette persuaded her to select her favorites and strategically place them in albums.

As she sat on the sofa, an album was in her lap. With each page turn, she reflected on her past. Even if the photographs glued on the pages were highlights, they brought memories to the surface. There were a lot of good ones, but some were not. The mere presence of smiles on the faces of the individuals in the photographs did not actually suggest that they were real. Dana spent the morning reviewing her life's history, but at some point, the physical memories ceased to exist.

Digital photography's inception. It changed the way individuals documented their life. Even if Dana had children, she would not have anything to pass on. *What? A memory card?*

At the conclusion of her photo album voyage, Dana took out her phone and browsed backwards through her photos. Many had been deleted throughout the years. Either as a result of failing technology or a change in Dana's attitude. Dana purged her life of Bridgette on the day the divorce was finalized, deleting her from her past and her phone. Those memories were no longer capable of eliciting tears from her. It was the absence of those images that activated the faucet that morning.

It was easier to press delete on the screen than to haul out a box of albums and tear up years of memories. In this manner, Dana's past stayed sealed. What would Dana's recollections look like if she lived an additional twenty or thirty years? She did not want her existence to be reduced to a series of digital zeros and ones.

Dana lowered another box from the top shelf in the closet. Inside were the remaining cameras she owned. One of them contained a partially used roll of film. Dana cleaned the lens of her camera, inside and out, without even knowing if film still existed. It brought a contented smile to her face as she recalled her younger years, when she took the time to maintain her equipment.

She discovered information about a newly-made film by conducting an Internet search. She also looked up information on her camera to refresh her memory. Without batteries, the camera still functioned. What a concept. Dana took a photograph of Mr. Jinx without knowing whether the film on her camera had expired.

Due to her lack of interest in photography, she paid no attention to the camera businesses in her neighborhood. Dana had two photographic retail stores within a five-mile radius. Once the sun dawned and the city awoke, Dana set out to see these two locations. The diner from the previous night was to her left. Her focus shifted to the parking lot where three police vehicles were parked.

She recalled that Cynthia had mentioned that her

father always drank a cup of coffee before his shift. Dana came into the parking lot and parked near the entrance. If Cynthia were present, she would greet her and perhaps share that cup of coffee with her. Regardless, Dana still needed breakfast. She would have a bite to eat before continuing with her errands.

Mae from the previous night entered the diner and walked up to the podium. "Morning, sweetie. Are you here for Morales? Or you on your own?"

The bond Mae forged between herself, and Cynthia felt natural. She longed to be associated with someone. "I suppose this means she is at her usual booth?"

"Sure is," Mae replied.

"I'll see myself to her." Dana grinned as she walked to the back of the restaurant. As Dana circled the path, she noticed that Cynthia was not alone at her booth. She sat with two other police officers. One of them appeared to be a woman with a ponytail that hung down her back. The other might be either. The short hair in the rear didn't reveal much. Cynthia's eyes detected Dana's presence, and she looked up as Dana approached.

Before Dana could reach the table, Cynthia rose from her booth. They met midway down the path. Cynthia smiled warmly. "I assumed I'd be the one to pursue this."

"A cup of coffee isn't a date." Dana grinned before gazing over at the booth, where the two women peered over their shoulders at them. "Perhaps another time, given you're busy at the moment."

"I can send them away. If I don't take advantage of this chance, you might not come back again."

Dana giggled as she placed a hand on Cynthia's arm. "Don't do that. We can meet... say, tomorrow? You tell me when to show up."

"So, a date?" Cynthia smiled and insisted on formalizing their forthcoming meeting.

"Not a date. I won't show up if you call it a date."

"Fine. Typically, I arrive here around seven in the morning."

"Seven? So early?"

"We can make it seven tonight?"

"No! Fine. Tomorrow at seven in the morning, I'll be here." Dana shuddered at the idea. She normally awoke at that time to begin her morning routine. She'd have to get up around six.

"Excellent. So, it's a date." Cynthia erased the spoken words with a hand gesture. "I mean, a meeting over coffee that isn't a date."

They looked at each other with caring eyes until Dana caught another glimpse of the two women at the booth still watching them. "Well, tomorrow then. Today? Stay safe."

Dana turned and exited the restaurant. As she arrived at her vehicle and opened the door, she heard her name yelled. Dana whirled toward the diner to see Cynthia racing toward her in her police uniform. She furrowed her brow, perplexed as to the situation. As soon as Cynthia arrived at her side, she brought Dana's face to her own. She mashed her lips, firmly planted on Dana's for a powerful and dominate kiss.

Dana's weak knees prevented her from pushing her away. "Just in case I'm not safe," Cynthia murmured as she parted while remaining near to her.

Dana squeezed her lips together as she inhaled Cynthia's patchouli fragrance. "That's not how you win me over."

"It's life. If tomorrow doesn't come, at least I'll have kissed you. There is no certainty. Besides, you might change your mind." Cynthia lowered her hands and grazed them slowly over Dana's neck and chest.

At one point, Dana's dream did not feature any annoying donkey noises. The moment where they kissed and explored one another was still fresh in her memories. As much as she hated the repulsive sound emanating from her during sex, she wanted to experience the rest. The only way for her to break through the barrier she had erected was to give in to her worries. Dana leaned toward her and gently placed her lips on Cynthia's.

Upon their separation, Dana ran her thumb across Cynthia's lips. "I'll show up if you do."

With that, Dana got in her car and drove away. She would keep her word and return the following day for coffee, and only coffee.

When six o'clock rolled around, she loathed committing to their early morning coffee meeting. As she dragged herself from the bed, she grumbled. While she had hoped for another dream, none had materialized. Possibly that was wise. If she had another bad dream involving a donkey, she might not have wanted to meet up with Cynthia for coffee at all.

Just before seven, Dana pulled into the parking lot and parked next to the lone police car. Inside the diner, Mae gave her a friendly greeting. "Morning, sweetie. She is waiting for you. I'll bring you a menu shortly."

"Oh, I'll just have coffee. Black. Thank you," she said. Dana took the initiative to round the tables and booths toward the rear, where she found Cynthia at her usual booth. Cynthia rose up to meet her with a wave.

Dana's chest constricted as she approached Cynthia at the table, causing her to flush. Both of them were unsure about how to respond to the awkward welcome, so they danced around a straightforward hello kiss. When Cynthia motioned for Dana to sit, they both chuckled. "Please. Thank you for coming."

Dana joked, "I'm glad you're alive."

Mae brought two mugs and a pot of coffee to the table. She poured a cup for each of them. "Have you eaten? Let me fetch you some eggs."

"No, but I'm good," Cynthia said.

Mae expressed a motherly concern. It was something that Dana remembered hearing from her own mother. "Nonsense. I'll wrestle you up some. You and your father are just too much alike."

When Mae walked away, Cynthia said, "Do you and Mae know each other outside of this place?"

Cynthia leaned on the table and clasped her hands in front of her. "You can say that. She was my father's mistress. Did not learn about it till after his death. I think we all knew that he came here every day for a reason. Made sense. Apparently, he talked a lot about us, so she knew about us but didn't know us well."

"Did finding out bother you?" Dana asked, taking a taste of the amazingly strong and very black coffee.

She leaned back, at ease in her own skin. "At first, yes. We resented her for taking him from the family. Except for me, nobody took the time to figure out why. My mother and him, it turns out, were not married. She fell out of love with him early on. He stayed nevertheless, hoping to win her back. He gave up at some point, but he never left."

"It sounds like a man who was devoted to his family."

"Family is everything. Like I stated, mine is fairly huge. How about you?"

Dana pulled her lips inward. "My mother is currently in Tampa. I have a brother and sister in Tampa as well, but neither of them is married or has children. My brother might have a few, but we don't know who they are. Mom was an only child, therefore we had no aunts or uncles. It's pretty much me."

"I have plenty for both of us." Cynthia grinned.

"You already seem to be lumping me in with the family."

"No. That would cause you to turn and run in the opposite direction. With Latinos, everyone is family. It isn't about blood. A family is built on honor and respect."

Then, an unnerving silence ensued. Dana didn't know where to take the conversation, so she fidgeted with her coffee mug. She watched the liquid swirl until she felt the morning going downhill quickly. They had nothing to say to one another.

Dana looked up, prepared to bid farewell. When she did so, Cynthia grinned and exhaled deeply. "I've always thought your eyes were stunning."

They dropped back down to the table. Her cheeks became flushed. She shook her head and remained silent since she did not know what to say. Cynthia added, "It's what drew me to you. I saw you a few times outside of the bar, here and there. Every time, the only thing I noticed about you was your eyes. My cousin insisted over and over that I ask you out at the bar."

Her eyebrows arched in a curious way, which led to the question. "Who is your cousin?"

"Jess. The bartender?"

"Wow. Do you know how many lesbians want her in the sack?"

"Probably the same number as the men who do it."

Bringing up Jess diverted the conversation from the subject of Dana's eyes. She disliked praises, especially those pertaining to her appearance. Partially self-conscious, Dana considered herself average. She is unremarkable, yet there was nothing terribly wrong with her. She looked at Cynthia's face and couldn't figure out what this beautiful woman saw in her. Cynthia could easily have a woman like Jess.

Once more, they felt the unease of silence. Cynthia's police radio broke the awkwardness between them. She removed the microphone from her shoulder and spoke police business into it, which sounded like gibberish to Dana.

Cynthia grabbed her wallet from her pocket and placed some dollars on the table. "I gotta run. I'm sorry."

"No. No worries." As she slid off the booth, Dana remarked, "Duty calls." Cynthia was already up when Dana stood up.

They left together. Dana matched Cynthia's quick stride to her police car. At the car, Cynthia offered, "I'll ask you again, would you like to join me for dinner? Tonight? Tomorrow? Anytime this month?"

Dana gave a headshake. "No. I'm not dating. And do not say that it is only dinner. Now, go to work and be careful!"

"I'd like to kiss you again."

She retreated, preventing Cynthia from attempting another kiss. Dana shouted from her vehicle's door. "Stay safe, Cynthia."

When six o'clock rolled around again, Dana did not grumble when she awoke. She washed, got dressed, and drove to the diner to meet Cynthia for coffee. Even though she didn't know if Cynthia would be there, the sight of the lone police car warmed her heart. Once more, she parked next to it and walked into the diner.

Mae's friendly smile greeted her like an old friend. Mae stated, "She's in the rear," knowing Dana had come for Cynthia.

As Dana turned the corner, she noticed a set of hands holding a newspaper upright. She had not thought Cynthia to be a reader of the news, but she knew so little about her. Dana slipped into the booth opposite her without uttering a word.

Slowly, and with a troubled frown, Cynthia lowered the page. When she realized Dana had returned for coffee, she smiled broadly and folded the page. "I must be doing something right if you have gotten up for me two days in a row."

She pretended to rise to her feet. Dana started to get up, hands on the table, and asked, "Do you want me to leave?"

"No. "Absolutely not!" Cynthia threw the newspaper aside and signaled service to Mae. "How has your morning been thus far?"

Mae joined them and poured a cup of tea for Dana, commenting, "You two make a nice couple."

"No," interjected Dana. "We're not together. Just friends."

Mae replenished Cynthia's cup as well before leaving, saying, "Well, you should be." The incident amused Cynthia.

"You paid her to say that, right? Convince her to give us a compliment?"

As she laughed, Cynthia swore, "No! I'd never do something like that."

"Just a little too convenient for my taste." Dana kept a straight face, but the way Cynthia insisted, she believed her.

"Seriously. I wouldn't do that. Not that I disagree with her, though. I think we'd make a good couple."

"I should go."

"No, please don't." Cynthia reached out and took Dana's hand in her own. "Since I cannot take you out and you refuse to eat dinner with me, this is the only way I can get to know you. Let's get to know each other. No strings. Zero expectations."

So, they drank coffee. Each day throughout that week and the following week, Dana awoke at six a.m. and drove to the coffee shop to see Cynthia. They shared stories, which made it easier for Dana to be herself because she didn't have to worry about trying to win someone over or wishing they would like her. Dana had not seen Cynthia do anything bizarre. This boded well, but they had only met at the dinner. There were no more dreams about donkeys. She could only hear the sound in her head whenever she envisaged the two of them becoming intimate with one another.

As they said their goodbyes at the car on Friday, Cynthia said, "I'll be at the bar tonight. If you show up by chance, I'll buy you a drink." She held out her hands, defending her words. "It's just one drink."

Dana chewed the inside of her lower lip as she slapped Cynthia on the arm.

"What?" Cynthia asked.

"Tell me something. What's wrong with you?"

The question made Cynthia wonder. "What does that mean? There's nothing wrong with me."

"You can't be perfect."

Cynthia laughed. "I'm far from perfect."

"Then what's wrong with you?"

She shook her head as she opened her police vehicle. "I'm going to go. Like I said, I am going to the bar. If I see you, say hello."

Cynthia drove away. She hadn't planned to spend the evening in the pub. To commemorate her fifty-fifth birthday, she intended to take herself out to dinner. She woke up to a birthday text message from Bridgette, just like she had done every year since they broke up. It was out of the question to bring up her birthday with Cynthia. She would keep that news a secret because she didn't want anything special from her. Things were going well, and she had a good friend. Since Cynthia hadn't said anything about it that morning, Dana was sure she didn't know.

Michelle and Scott hadn't been heard from in a while. She gave them time to calm down after they abruptly left her open house. She thought that if they didn't check in with her on that day, they probably hated her. Dana noticed the passive-aggressive behavior, but she didn't change it. That day wasn't the time to apologize. It made her look desperate for attention.

Around lunchtime, the door to the shop opened. Dana's hands were full with a bouquet, but she peered around the corner anyhow. Michelle presented a gift from their favorite bakery, much to her astonishment. "I come bearing oatmeal cream pies for someone's birthday."

"You don't hate me?" Dana asked, as she motioned Michelle back.

"Of course not. In all honesty, I've had to deal with my moronic brother and his girlfriend. Trust me, no one needs their crap in their lives. However, enough of that! Happy birthday, you ol' bitch!"

"Thanks. And the thought of that cream pie is heavenly. Have you spoken with Scott? He has also been missing since that night. I honestly thought I had lost you two."

Michelle laughed at the notion. "Did you truly believe we would break up over a woman?"

"Some woman that I'm kind of falling for," Dana cringed at the thought. Not at Cynthia, but rather at the notion of falling in love

Michelle responded as she opened the bag and retrieved two pairs of oatmeal cookies filled to the brim with fluffy cream. "You make it sound like a bad thing. I thought that's what you were looking for."

"It's just... odd."

"Are we discussing the lady from the open house? The hot one?"

"Yes. Her. Cynthia. Every morning before she starts work, I meet her for coffee. She's a lovely lady. Funny. Kind."

"Hot," Michelle added.

"She's very pretty. I'll admit."

"So what is her problem? You find something flawed in every person."

"Nothing. That's what makes it strange. Even Bridgette had a list of flaws that I ignored."

"So what are you saying? She is perfect for you?"

"Stop," insisted Dana. "We've only had coffee. We have not actually been out. We haven't hooked up yet, so I'm fairly sure it will be terrible when we get there."

"When you get there? So, sex is most certainly on the table?"

"Rephrase. If. If we get that far."

"You need to lighten up and let things unfold naturally, honey."

"You're probably right. She's really nice."

"There you have it. Now, let's discuss this evening. We are going out, right? I see some liquor in our future."

Dana laughed excessively hard. Michelle wanted to take her drinking. Because they frequented the same bar, Cynthia would be there. It was her special day. She should enjoy life more. What's the harm in simply letting go and seeing what happened? "Fine. Let's do it."

"Perfect. I'll meet you at your house, and we can take an Uber. We can drink until hair grows on our chests."

"Whatever. I'll be ready."

Michelle arrived at Dana's residence that evening at seven o'clock. They called a car to pick them up and rode to their favorite bar, a place they had frequented for years prior to Dana's divorce. As they pulled up to the curb, Dana tried to recall over the years why she missed Cynthia. As regulars, they encountered many of the same individuals, whether or not they spoke. She couldn't place Cynthia before the night she got drunk.

She had made a fool of herself that night and dreaded entering the bar and seeing Jess, who had cut her off after too much drinking. If she hadn't thought Cynthia might be inside, she might have asked Michelle to take her somewhere else. Michelle opened the door for Dana at the front entrance.

Instantaneously, the entire bar exclaimed, "Happy Birthday!"

Dana jumped back. The sight of so many people wishing her a happy birthday caused her to nearly shed a tear. As people applauded and cheered for her, Michelle pushed her forward. Dana's cheeks turned bright red at the unexpected recognition. Scott's presence at the bar made her feel loved, even though she disliked being the center of attention. He ran up to her and embraced her in a bear hug.

Dana smiled and addressed her friends, "You guys. "I love you, but you did not have to do all of this."

Michelle whispered while leaning in close to her. "We had nothing to do with this."

Dana took a quick look at the bar's decorations, which included streamers, a huge banner hanging above the bar, and latex balloons in various colors. As her eyes admired all the celebratory mementos, she spotted the beautiful woman responsible for all of them. Cynthia shrugged and smirked in response to Dana's smile.

Michelle and Scott left her side, and Dana strolled over to where Cynthia leaned arrogantly against the counter. It could have been her one and only flaw; the one thing Dana saw in Cynthia that ultimately doomed them. That cocky grin. Cynthia's arrogance. She would have to accept it because it made Dana desire her even more. She closed the distance between them by placing her hands on Cynthia's chest and kissing her so passionately that the entire room fell silent.

It surprised Cynthia as much as it did everyone else, because when she pulled back a little, Cynthia caught her breath and said, "Happy birthday?"

"Thank you." Dana responded so quietly that only Cynthia could hear her.

"The first drink is on me. What can I get you?"

Dana crafted a seductive smile. "I'd like to say you, but I'll take a glass of chardonnay."

For a while, they didn't look away from one

another, almost daring the other to give them another kiss. Cynthia finally closed her eyes and turned to wave down Jess.

"Happy birthday," Jess said when she reached them. "What are we getting the birthday girl?"

"Thanks," Dana said.

"Chardonnay for the lady, and I'll take beer," Cynthia continued.

"Coming up," Jess said as she moved away to get their drinks.

"Hmm, you actually pulled this off, huh? All of it? And how exactly did you find out it was my birthday? I didn't tell you."

"Misuse of power. The night you had too much to drink, I checked you out. Don't be upset. I wanted to make sure you got home safely."

"I'm not upset, but how did you know I'd show up?"

Cynthia nodded. "I hoped you would like me enough to accept my offer, and I also secured it by getting in touch with your friend over there."

She meant Michelle. Dana cast an eye over Michelle and Scott, who were already firing off a round of shots at the bar. She grinned and nodded, "I would have shown up without her."

"Nice to know. Does that mean you'll finally go out with me?"

Dana shook her head. "No. I don't date, but if you're willing to go all in, I'd love to be in love with you, give up these stupid dating apps, and—"

Cynthia silenced her by kissing the birthday girl

passionately and taking her into her arms. As they shared their first official kiss as a couple, she lifted Dana off the ground in a huge hug. "I'm officially off the market!" she yelled at the bar after Cynthia let her down.

As Jess set their drinks down on the counter, the customers laughed and applauded. "Congratulations, Cousin! Dana, welcome to the family."

"We're not getting married," Dana said with a shake of her head.

Jess winked. "Yet. Still, everyone is family."

"Yet?" Dana chuckled. She shook her head and shot Cynthia another icy stare. "Yet?"

"You said you don't date. What else is there?"

When Dana reached for the chardonnay, she caught sight of the glass and saw a ring at the bottom of the drink. "Cynthia? No."

"Are you really saying no?"

Dana's lips pressed together. Her heart grew heavier with love as her chest constricted around it. Her head shook. While she did not respond negatively, she did not respond at all.

"I'm not perfect, but I'm all in. This feels just so natural for some strange reason. I want to see you every morning at six o'clock, but not at the coffee shop. In bed and waking up to you. Here is the craziness you keep saying you find. Exactly this. Dana, this is my crazy. You."

Not saying no. Saying nothing. She continued to shake her head while pleading with her eyes not to cry.

# DANA

Dana awoke from a deep slumber when she felt a cold, wet nose on her cheek. She turned her head to the other side of the bed, shooed Mr. Jinx away, and slowly opened her eyes. Empty. Dana didn't like waking up by herself, but it did happen. She dragged herself out of bed and shuffled her way through the bedroom, down the hall, and into the kitchen.

The aroma of freshly brewed coffee made her smile, as did wrapping her arms around the already dressed woman leaning against the counter, reading a newspaper. Dana inhaled as she took a whiff of her favorite patchouli cologne. "Sexy morning. Why did you let me sleep in?"

Cynthia dropped the paper on the counter, slid her arms around, and placed hers on Dana's small of her back. Like usual, their morning began with a passionate kiss. "It's your birthday and a day of pampering, so you should sleep in."

"Jinx, unlike someone I know, wanted me up for some kisses." Dana struck Cynthia in the butt before moving on to pour a cup of coffee.

Cynthia leapt in front of her and snatched the mug out of her grasp. "I'll get that for you. Pampering. Remember."

"Whatever." Cynthia poured a cup of coffee as Dana leaned against the counter. "I don't see you staying home and taking care of everything for me. When I need a few seconds, should I call you?"

"And thirds, and fourths. Trust me, if this meeting wasn't required, I'd be here, and we'd still be in bed." Cynthia leaned in and kissed Dana in the crook of her neck. Cynthia added, with her lips on Dana's skin, "Making love to you all day long."

Cynthia's flirtatious and seductive invitation to the bedroom made Dana chuckle. "What time is your meeting?"

She reluctantly retracted as she took a quick look at her watch. "Soon. I've got to run. The spa is at ten; don't forget it." Cynthia patted herself down to ensure she had everything she needed. With a final kiss before rushing out the door, she said, "Happy Birthday, babe. I love you."

"Love you too." Dana swatted Cynthia on the butt one last time as she dashed to the front door.

A warmth in her heart brought a smile to her face as she celebrated another birthday. So much had happened in the previous year, and her morning would be filled with all the memories she recorded along the way.

Dana settled into the sofa with her mug in hand. There was a photo album on the coffee table in front of her. Next to it were packs of processed film and prints. Everything she'd accumulated over the year was in front of her. She ran her fingers over the album's bejeweled cover, smiling at the words: *CYNTHIA AND*

*DANA - YEAR 1.*

In chronological order, Dana opened each pack of prints. She went through them and chose her favorite ones. Photos from her 55th birthday were in the first stack. She flipped through the photos of her friends laughing and celebrating, though one of the last few pictures on that roll was taken after the party. Photographs of Cynthia straddling Dana while she glared seductively into the camera. While the photos were not explicit, Dana remembered they were naked and had already consummated their relationship. The final photograph pictured Jinx sniffing their toes. She removed her favorites and placed them among the album's pages.

Roll after roll allowed Dana to relive the special moments she shared with Cynthia. Thanksgiving with Cynthia's family made for some wonderful photo opportunities. Then Cynthia's large family and her small family celebrated Christmas together. The holidays brought the entire family together, but New Year's became much more than just a time to ring in the new year. They tied the knot.

Dana never imagined getting married again. Hell, she never even imagined finding love after the year she had. Instead, it found her. A woman who instilled craziness in her. A woman who discovered an adventurous sprint she had no idea existed. Cynthia not only loved her, but she never doubted that they were meant to be together. It was a small gathering —Latin Cynthia's family never did anything small. The photos she'd treasure for many moons to come.

Throughout the evening, Dana photographed her loved ones celebrating their special occasion.

The next envelope contained a series of photos of Cynthia and her police colleagues walking through the flower shop door on Valentine's Day after the delivery company failed to show up. They rescued her, and Dana documented everything she could. A physical memory she could touch.

The rolls included pictures from Cynthia's birthday. They made a special journey up Florida's east coast on a motorcycle. Dana had photos of the scenery as well as touristy photos that she had others take of them.

After that joyful moment came the one Dana dreaded. Scott's memorial service and vigil for the victims of yet another hate crime against the queer community. Without Cynthia, she might not have survived what was one of the hardest days of her life. She had never been more terrified in her life as she watched the news unfold and knew that her wife was working overtime and managing the carnage. When Cynthia entered her home shortly after dawn, Dana learned that Scott was among the victims of the shooting. Dana sobbed uncontrollably. Cynthia's firm and supportive embrace helped her get through the heartbreaking news. Dana documented the community's outpouring of love and acceptance in the days and weeks following the shooting as people gathered to remember the victims.

As she placed a photo of Scott in the photo album, Dana wiped a tear from her eye. It took a considerable amount of time to turn the page as she recalled all of the wonderful times, she had shared with him. When she did, Dana found another wonderful and joyful memory when she opened the next package of prints. Michelle's baby shower.

In the midst of everything, Michelle hooked up with one of Cynthia's numerous cousins. Even though Michelle claimed she wasn't dating Rico, the two of them spent a lot of time together after the shower. Coincidentally, that day was the baby's due date. Of all days, Dana's birthday. Michelle wasn't completely certain it would happen though. Dana, who was married to a family of betters, had a lot riding on her lucky day. Dana would take the money and put it away for her Goddaughter's future if by chance the baby girl showed up that day.

Dana filled the photo album from cover to cover with more birthdays and other special occasions. It would be the first of numerous albums that would chronicle her new life, which she treasured above all else. As she put the album away and set it on the table, she took a quick look around the house to take in the variety of cultures and personalities. It might have bothered Dana to not have everything perfectly matched and designed when she lived with Bridgette, but she didn't mind with Cynthia. It was their house; one they had created jointly.

Mr. Jinx leaped onto the table and rubbed the photo album with his face. Dana stroked his head and said, "Yeah, buddy. I adore our family as well."

It was time for a quick shower before her spa

appointment. Michelle's birthday present, which she desperately needed. Dana threw on some yoga pants and a tight-fitting sports shirt, then snatched her keys and sped off in her car. She received a call from Michelle as soon as she entered the parking lot.

Quick to react, Dana asked, "Are you okay? Is it time?"

"I'm on my way to the hospital right now." Michelle sighed into the phone. "This little girl is coming whether I like it or not.

Dana's voice grew louder, and her speech became more rapid. "Okay. I'm on my way as well. I'll text Cynthia to meet us there after she finishes her meeting. Hold your legs together until I arrive."

"Yeah. Like it'd help. Just get your ass over there," Michelle demanded before the phone disconnected.

She had to remain calm. As she messaged Cynthia, her elation over the birth of the baby accelerated her typing speed. *Baby, Mama's in labor. Headed to hospital. Meet me there when you're done.*

Dana slammed the car into drive and sped out of the parking lot, skipping her appointment. Dana swerved in and out of traffic until she arrived at the hospital while still driving safely. When Dana rushed in and pushed her way to the desk, her wife's worried eyes greeted her instead of the smiling receptionist.

Cynthia took Dana's clammy hands into hers, raising Dana's pulse. "What? What's going on?"

"There are some issues. I hurried over after Rico called. They were forced to perform an emergency C-section. We must wait outside." Cynthia tried to calm her down, but it didn't work.

"Where is she? I need to be there!"

Cynthia drew Dana close as she hushed her. "You can't. We wait and trust that everything will be fine. Let's go."

She took Dana to the side, and they waited for updates. Cynthia's uniform must have made it appear much worse to everyone in the lobby with a police officer calming a woman in distress. Dana found solace in feeling the bulletproof vest's thickness. When Scott died, she remembered that strength. With Michelle in surgery, she needed it more than ever.

"She will be fine," Cynthia said in her ear as they sat next to each other. "Michelle is a bad ass and is stubborn as hell. Plus, the baby has Morales blood. We're fighters."

They waited there for a few hours before Rico finally emerged, grinning. Despite seeing his joy, Dana still rushed to him in a panic. "Tell me they're okay!"

"It's a girl! Michelle is doing fine. They're both doing well, but still recovering. And she's so fucking adorable," Rico exclaimed with a broad grin.

"See. I told you to have faith in the Morales blood." Cynthia drew Dana into her embrace, wrapping her arm around her and kissing the side of her head.

Rico led them to the viewing area where they were able to see the newborn baby. The sign read Morales. It didn't take long for the Morales family to overrun the hospital. Members of their large family came around one by one to see the baby. They congregated outside, with everyone wishing Rico luck. Dana strayed away from the group and headed for Michelle's bedroom.

She peered inside to figure out whether the mother had awakened. The adorable infant girl rested in Michelle's arms while her eyes were open. "Are you open to visitors?"

Michelle's voice cracked as she asked, "You? Of course. Come see this little one."

Dana entered quietly, trying to be as quiet as possible. "She has your face."

"Who knew I could do this?" Michelle wondered aloud, looking down at her chest to the sleeping baby.

"I did. Scott knew you could, too. Have you settled on a name yet?"

"I have. Scottie. He would have made the coolest uncle."

Dana wiped the tear from her cheek before reaching over to Michelle's face to do the same for hers. "That is the best name ever. You know I never would have downloaded that stupid app or met Cynthia if it weren't for him. You never would've met Rico. And this little angel wouldn't be here right now. So, Scottie is a perfect name."

Dana took out her jacket's pocket camera and snapped a photo of Scottie and her mother. "Here's the first photo for the start of year two," Dana said as she removed the camera from her eye.

After giving Scottie a head kiss, she leaned over and kissed Michelle. Dana felt Cynthia's hand gently brush her shoulders as she stood up. Dana inhaled deeply as she felt more love in that room than she had ever experienced in her entire life. She was proud of her family. She wouldn't have wanted to be anywhere else.

FIN

# THANK YOU

Thank you for taking the time to read SWIPE
RIGHT FOR LOVE. I hope you enjoyed it as much as I
enjoyed writing it. Please leave a review on Amazon
or Goodreads; I'd love to hear your thoughts.

For more information on Cyan LeBlanc, please
visit the website www.posiesandpeacocks.com

# MORE BOOKS BY CYAN LEBLANC

Open Your Eyes

Cause & Effect

The Queen and I

Funeral of A Good Girl

Printed in Great Britain
by Amazon

20983487R00172